JHY
S

Alternate Voices in the Contemporary Latin American Narrative

Alternate Voices

in the Contemporary Latin American Narrative

David William Foster

University of Missouri Press
Columbia, 1985

Copyright © 1985 by
The Curators of the University of Missouri
University of Missouri Press, Columbia, Missouri, 65211
Printed and bound in the United States of America

Library of Congress Cataloging in Publication Data

Foster, David William.
    Alternate voices in the contemporary Latin American
narrative.

    Bibliography: p.
    Includes index.
    1. Latin American prose literature—20th century—
History and criticism.   I. Title.
PQ7082.P76F67   1985   868'.08   85–1411
ISBN 0-8262-0481-3

∞™ This paper meets the minimum requirements of
the American National Standard for Permanence of Paper
for Printed Library Materials, Z39.48, 1984.

To my students,
the best audience a scholar can have.

Contents

Acknowledgments

Versions of two of these essays have appeared previously in print: Chapter 1 in *PMLA* 99 (1984), and Chapter 3 in *Chasqui* 10, i (1980). Some of the individual sections of Chapters 3 and 4 involve the extensive rewriting of review notes that appeared originally in *Chasqui, World Literature Today, Latin American Digest,* and *Hispamérica.* The section on María Luisa Mendoza in Chapter 4 appeared in Spanish as "Algunos espejismos eróticos" in *Plural* 37 (1984):36–38. A version of Chapter 2 also appears in *Woman as Myth and Metaphor in Latin American Literature,* edited by Carmelo Virgillo and Naomi Lindstrom (University of Missouri Press, 1985).

All translations not otherwise credited are my own.

This project began originally with funding from Arizona State University's Faculty Grant-in-Aid Program to study sociopolitical commitment in the contemporary Argentine novel.

D.W.F.
Tempe, Ariz.
June 1985

Preface

One of the most interesting and challenging contemporary cultural debates is the one termed *Orientalism*.[1] By referring to Western ways of creating a self-serving image of the "east," Orientalism implies a consciousness whereby scholars may question the primacy of the Western point of view, at least as it has prevailed historically as synonymous with universal standards and the height of cultural accomplishment.

While Western cultural imperialism has tended to interpret other cultures either as primitive stages that will be set aside in favor of the apex of civilization or as quaintly exotic traditions that may have the right to exist outside the dominant orbit, the study of Orientalism can help us to decentralize the discussion of culture and to recognize how the ideologies of cultural definitions blind us to the principles of foreign cultures and prevent us from assessing the often irreconcilable goals that separate cultures. Intellectuals like Edward Said, whose study on Orientalism is considered one of the major statements on the subject,[2] are concerned with both the general issues of cultural description and the more immediate issue of how Western societies have been incapable of understanding political movements in the Third World because they see the latter only in terms of their own cultural ideology and its inherent bad faith toward non-Western "Orientals."[3]

The student of Latin American culture is, not surprisingly, particularly responsive to the issues raised by Said and others in this regard. In many respects, Latin America is a constellation of Western societies. Yet we may count as essentially Third

1. There are numerous reviews of the subject in the cultural press. See, for example, the negative assessment by Bernard Lewis, "The Question of Orientalism," *New York Review of Books* 29, xi (1982):49–56; and the rejoinder by Edward Said et al. to Lewis, "Orientalism: An Exchange," *New York Review of Books* 29, xiii (1982):44–48.
2. Edward Said, *Orientalism* (New York: Pantheon Books, 1978).
3. Michel Foucault is another thinker who, in his study of the "archaeology of knowledge," also contributes to deconstructing the presumed universals of Western knowledge. See his *L'Archéologie du savoir* (Paris: Gallimard, 1969).

World concerns its economic and political identification with noncapitalist issues, the uniqueness of its pre-Columbian heritage on the one hand and its Spanish roots on the other (roots that extend back to a time when Spain was on the periphery of Western Europe), and the generally felt need among Latin American creative figures to elaborate a national and/or regional culture not dependent on definitions emanating from the "colonial" or "imperial" centers.

The history of the attempts at Latin American national and regional identity is a long and complex one that cannot be rehearsed here.[4] Suffice it to say that even today it is impossible to discern any unanimity among intellectuals and artists as to whether or not the concept of Latin America refers to a unified—or desirably unifiable—regional culture or merely bespeaks certain common historical roots and the general position of the Latin American republics in the framework of the dominant cultural centers. The contribution of a sensitivity toward the issues of Orientalism or toward Third-World thought in general (as vague as the whole notion of the Third World may be from a more doctrinaire Marxist position) has been to make the student of Latin America aware of the dangers—or at least the ideological implications—of continuing to define Latin American phenomena in terms of models that may be foreign to those phenomena or may not be fully adequate to describe them. In other words, this means not inventorying Latin American literature in terms of the categories developed for American or French or some other culturally prestigious literature.[5]

A considerable number of critics have noted that the so-called boom in Latin American fiction in the sixties and early seventies may have been due more to foreign perceptions of Latin American literature than to any internal features of the

4. One programmatic series of attempts to define culture through literature is the compilation directed by César Fernández Moreno, *América latina en su literatura* (Mexico City: Siglo XXI; Paris: UNESCO, 1972). Significantly, this volume is part of the incomplete series "América latina en su cultura."
5. Perhaps black culture has presented the most complex problems in terms of its place in schemes of Latin American culture. See the introductory chapter by Richard L. Jackson, "The Problems of Literary Blackness in Latin America," in his *Black Writers in Latin America* (Albuquerque: University of New Mexico Press, 1979). There is, of course, a fairly extensive bibliography on Caribbean black literature.

literature.[6] A variant of this position might argue that the boom was the result of the calculated appeal by certain writers and their agents to potential foreign interests. In this view, a Latin American literary phenomenon resulted from the implicit appeal to the structures of cultural domination rather than from an attempt to develop a specifically Latin American fictional tradition. The debate cannot be settled through any sort of scientific proof, and no real contribution to the matter is made by affirming that the boom was both a truly Latin American phenomenon and the result of clever international marketing. The abiding issue, rather, is to recognize the ideological assumptions made by the critics who see the boom as pandering to the interests of cultural domination, as well as the assumptions made by those who see the works involved as the definitive maturation of the Latin American novel allowing it to compete successfully on the international scene.

Among Latin American critics, there is considerable opposition to continuing to study Spanish American and Brazilian literature in terms of categories and genres, movements, and schools identified on the basis of foreign models, primarily French, British, and American. Roberto Fernández Retamar and Desiderio Navarro in Cuba, Carlos Rincón in Colombia, and even José Carlos Mariátegui in Peru over fifty years ago have been important figures in the discussion of how to describe adequately the literature of Latin America without simply seeing it in terms of dominant models.[7] As Navarro has written, it is not so much a question of ignoring the critical and theoretical models of the prestige cultures or of insisting that

6. This is essentially the position of Hernán Vidal in *Literatura hispanoamericana e ideología liberal: surgimiento y crisis (una problemática sobre la dependencia en torno a la narrativa del boom)*. I consider the best survey of the ideological issues of criticism on the boom to be the study by Angel Rama, "El 'boom' en perspectiva."

7. Roberto Fernández Retamar, *Para una teoría de la literatura hispanoamericana* (Havana: Casa de las Américas, 1976); 2d ed. (Mexico City: Nuestro Tiempo, 1977); Desiderio Navarro, "Eurocentrismo y antieurocentrismo en la teoría literaria de América latina y Europa," *Revista de crítica literaria latinoamericana* 16 (1982):7–26; Carlos Rincón, *El cambio de la noción de literatura* (Bogotá: Andes, 1978); José Carlos Mariátegui, *Siete ensayos de interpretación de la realidad peruana* (Lima: Amauta, 1928). See also the position papers by Fernando Alegría, Noé Jitrik, Rafael Gutiérrez Girardot, Marta Traba, and Angel Rama in *Literatura y praxis en América latina* (Caracas: Monte Avila Editores, 1974), and the papers on the novel in *Literatura latinoamericana e ideología de la dependencia, Hispamérica* Anejo I (1975).

a discussion of literary universals be halted until inductive cultural histories can be written of all societies. Rather, an awareness of the ideology underlying scholarly approaches can help us use them with care and supplement and complement them as appropriate for the material under discussion. In the case of the contemporary Latin American novel, there is no question that many of the historical surveys are subservient to criteria that are extrinsically definable. For example, Leo Pollman's work in French ties the Latin American novel to the French new novel.[8] The monographs in English by Gordon Brotherston, John S. Brushwood, and the considerable material published in the English-language nonacademic press are essentially concerned with the Latin American works that have most attracted attention in their translation into English.[9] Donald L. Shaw's survey in Spanish is more comprehensive in that he does not focus only on the Latin American novel in English translation.[10] However, it is remarkable that, even as Shaw sets out to provide a more balanced portrait, no women writers are included. Moreover, it is routine to speak of Latin American fiction with reference only to works in Spanish, as though Brazil's extensive and impressive tradition of the novel and short story were not part of Latin America.[11]

*　*　*

The chapters in this volume are contributions toward a reassessment of contemporary Latin American writing and are based on the strategy of willfully imposing a perspective at radical variance with the existing bibliography on the subject. By eschewing the approach of a historical overview, by focusing on works that are not predominantly available in English translation, by choosing categories that do not evoke prevailing literary norms, and by concentrating on writings that rashly juxtapose well-known works with relatively unknown ones, I

8. Leo Pollman, La "nueva novela" en Francia y en Iberoamérica (Madrid: Gredos, 1971).

9. Gordon Brotherston, The Emergence of the Latin American Novel (Cambridge: Cambridge University Press, 1977); John S. Brushwood, The Spanish American Novel: A Twentieth Century Survey.

10. Donald L. Shaw, Nueva narrativa hispanoamericana (Madrid: Cátedra, 1981).

11. However, the Twayne World Author Series survey on the Latin American Short Story, edited by Margaret Sayers Peden (Boston: G. K. Hall, 1982), includes, as one of its four chapters, a study on Brazilian fiction by the author of the present monograph.

hope both to suggest a more comprehensive (although necessarily fragmentary) panorama of Latin American fiction and to suggest a consideration of works on the basis of criteria other than their "international stature" or the extent to which they represent Spanish-language variations on modalities whose importance has been established by French or American example.[12] For example, my first chapter deals with documentary narrative in Latin America. Although the nonfiction narrative has a certain prominence in English, I contend that it is both an integral part of contemporary Latin American writing, and, in fact, symptomatic of the goals of the Latin American writer. By contrast, my second chapter focuses on a work that is not a novel at all or even arguably a narrative. Eva Perón's *La razón de mi vida* can, nevertheless, be read in terms of the conventions of a certain type of popular literature. My reason for including it, however, is neither to assimilate it to a novelistic canon nor to argue for its assessment as an important literary document. Rather, by such a controversial choice, I wish to stress how, in terms of modern theoretical postulates and in view of the need to see Latin American literature apart from Western priorities, the distinction between literature and nonliterature, between narrative and nonnarrative, between narrative and political tract, is a tenuous one that does not significantly contribute to our estimation of writing in Latin America.[13]

Chapter Three is perhaps more conventional in that it focuses on a series of works that are clearly fictional and unquestionably novelistic. But more important than the fact that only one is by an author known in English (Manuel Puig) is their pertinence to a scheme of countercultural writing in Argentina that essentially insures that they will not be translated. By engaging in a demythification of Buenos Aires and by making use

12. A publication like *Review* (1968–), of the Center for Inter-American Relations in New York, has had an admirable record of presenting a balanced image of Latin American culture in English. Particularly noteworthy are its Focus issues on specific topics and writers, both major figures well represented in translations (Borges, Pablo Neruda, Octavio Paz, for example) and those who have yet to become widely available in English (for example, a recent issue— no. 31—is devoted to the Argentine, Roberto Arlt [1900–1942], a touchstone writer barely known outside of Spanish; Naomi Lindstrom, who edited this issue, has recently translated Arlt's *The Seven Madmen* [New York: Robert Godine, 1984].)
13. This is one of the principal thrusts of Costanzo D. Girolamo, *A Critical Theory of Literature* (Madison: University of Wisconsin Press, 1981).

of intertextual allusions to the flotsam and jetsam of the cultural codes of Argentine society, it is likely that these novels could not appeal to foreign readers. The question remains whether or not they should, therefore, simply be ignored. On the other hand, I argue that they demand analysis because they exemplify what the Argentine novelist is doing irrespective of the external demand to write something that will appeal to the foreign reader in translation.

My final chapter investigates a series of novelistic modalities that have not received adequate scholarly attention either in Latin America or among foreign scholars. Nevertheless, they do define the parameters of novelistic practice in Latin America, parameters that do not necessarily jibe with practices in other areas of the world. For example, although there is a fine tradition of serious detective fiction and innovative science fiction in English, we find it difficult to believe that either form can be truly meaningful in Spanish. We are particularly surprised at the suggestion that **science** fiction can be meaningful in technologically underdeveloped societies. And, because we have no contemporary examples of major novelists also writing children's literature, literary scholars have ignored the texts by Latin American writers I refer to in this chapter.

Although this study does not "correct the balance"—it would be pretentious to attempt to—it does constitute a call for a less biased or skewed approach to Latin American literature. Put simply, we must cease to devote all our critical energies to Gabriel García Márquez and Jorge Luis Borges and concern ourselves with the other vast literary riches of Latin America. Some of them, upon examination, might not appear as unpertinent, as untranslatable, as we may have thought.

1. Latin American Documentary Narrative

Pero es que muchos se olvidan, con disfrazarse de magos a poco costo, que lo maravilloso comienza a serlo de manera inequívoca cuando surge de una revelación privilegiada de la realidad, de una iluminación inhabitual o singularmente favorecedora de las inadvertidas riquezas de la readidad, de una ampliación de las escalas y categoría de la realidad, percibidas con particular intensidad en virtud de una exaltación del espíritu que lo conduce a un modo de "estado límite."[1]

(But many forget, disguising themselves as cheap magicians, that the marvelous manifests itself unequivocally only when it derives from an unexpected alteration of reality (the miracle), from a privileged revelation of reality, from an unaccustomed or singularly advantageous illumination of the unnoticed richness of reality, from an amplification of the registers and categories of reality, perceived with a special intensity by virtue of an exaltation of the spirit, which it transports to a sort of "critical state.")

¿Pero qué es la historia de América toda sino una crónica de lo real-maravilloso?

(But what is the history of America if not a chronicle of the marvelous real?)

I

Alejo Carpentier's famous statement concerning the fabulous quality of Latin American reality, on which Gabriel García Márquez elaborated in his definitive novel of Latin America, *Cien años de soledad* (1967), possesses a double critical importance: it stresses the interpretation of spurious categories like empirical reality and imaginative fantasies, and it underscores by implication the continuity between documentary history and nar-

---

1. Alejo Carpentier, "De lo real maravillosamente americano," in his *Tientos y diferencias (ensayos)*, pp. 131–32; the second quotation is from p. 135.

1

rative fictions.[2] The simple fact is that contemporary Latin American fiction has been routinely characterized as predominantly a social testimonial. The scholar may resist tracing the narrative in terms of sociopolitical commentary from Domingo Faustino Sarmiento's *Facundo* (1848), on the Rosas dictatorship in Argentina, to Mariano Azuela's *Los de abajo* (1916), the most eloquent example of the novel of the Mexican Revolution of 1910. But there is little doubt that, first with the novels of social realism,[3] and then with contemporary fiction that bears witness to the conflict of Latin American society, there has been an emphasis on fiction as an especially productive form of documentary. Perhaps the most sustained example is the work of David Viñas, who for almost thirty years has been projecting a revisionist history of Argentine society in his novels.[4]

By the same token, there has been a recent abundance of novels concerning one of the key phenomena of Latin American society, the dictator.[5] Augusto Roa Bastos's *Yo el Supremo* (1975) is an outstanding example of these novels. Through the first-person narrative of Dr. José Gaspar Rodríguez de Francia (1766–1840), Paraguay's enlightened, utopian despot, the novel represents not only all the contradictions of early independent Latin America but also the entire liberal tradition up to the present day. In this sense, Roa's novel is the quintessential Latin American historical novel: it deals with the arbitrary violence and unremitting oppression of dictatorial regimes, it abounds in specific historical references and incorporates a wide range of explicit documentary materials, it surmounts mere chronological limitations in order to range over the entire

2. Virtually all the major studies on Latin American literature make this point. Fundamental are the essays in César Fernández Moreno, comp., *América latina en su literatura*, and Oscar Collazos and Julio Cortázar, *Literatura en la revolución y revolución en la literatura*. Miguel Barnet, one of the authors I examine in this study, establishes fundamental criteria in "La novela testimonio: socio-literatura," in his *La canción de Rachel*, pp. 125–50.

3. Social realism has yet to be studied adequately in Latin America. See, however, the monographs by Juan Carlos Portantiero, *Realismo y realidad en la narrativa argentina*; Harry L. Rosser, *Conflict and Transition in Rural Mexico: The Fiction of Social Realism*; and David William Foster, *Argentine Narrative of Social Realism* (unpublished).

4. See Emir Rodríguez Monegal, "David Viñas en su contorno," *Mundo nuevo* 18 (1967):75–86. Also in his *Narradores de esta América*, 2d ed. (Montevideo/Buenos Aires: Alfa, 1969–1974), 2:310–30.

5. Concerning the image of the dictator in the contemporary novel, see Jorge Castellanos and Miguel A. Martínez, "El dictador hispanoamericano como personaje literario."

span of Paraguayan and Latin American history, and it proceeds with a clear projection of the ideological problems of writing in a society in which vast segments of the population are illiterate and in which discourse is the privilege of a despotic elite (*dictator*, of course, derives from *dictare*, and the textual basis of the novel is Francia's act of dictating his memoirs).[6]

Thus, it would be an easy task to enumerate a lengthy list of contemporary Latin American works of fiction that novelize to one degree of documentary explicitness or another the specific facets of a complex Latin American society. Julio Cortázar's novel on revolutionary exiles, *El libro de Manuel* (1973), incorporates explicit documentary material on violence against the Third World. José Donoso's *Casa de campo* (1978) allegorizes the right-wing military coup in Chile in 1973. Edmundo Desnoes's *Memorias del subdesarrollo* (1965) portrays the tensions of revolutionary change in Cuba. Jorge Asís's *Los reventados* (1974) concerns Perón's "triumphal" return to Argentina in 1973 and is only one of a long line of Argentine novels dealing with the Peronista phenomenon.[7] Carlos Fuentes's *La cabeza de la hidra* (1978) uses a spy-novel mold to treat features of Mexico's emergence as an oil-rich superpower. The list could be extended almost indefinitely. Moreover, ample parallel examples from the contemporary Latin American theater could be adduced, particularly in the case of countries like Argentina, Cuba, Mexico, and Brazil, where there is an eloquent tradition of using the public spectacle of theater for sociopolitical information.[8]

With this wide array of literary materials, it is not surprising to discover a particularly impressive emphasis in Latin America on documentary or nonfiction narrative. Much has been written about the nonfiction novel in recent American literature, but the American nonfiction novel is fundamentally an outgrowth of the new journalism. While some big names like

6. See David William Foster, "Augusto Roa Bastos's *I the Supreme*: The Image of a Dictator," and Domingo Miliani, "El dictador: objeto narrativo en *Yo el Supremo*."
7. Consult the studies by Andrés Oscar Avellaneda, "El tema del peronismo en la narrativa argentina"; Ernesto Goldar, *El peronismo en la literatura argentina*; and Rodolfo A. Borello, "Novela e historia: la visión fictiva del período peronista en las letras argentinas."
8. For a sample of criticism on these dramatists, see the essays in Leon F. Lyday and George W. Woodyard, eds., *Dramatists in Revolt: The New Latin American Theater* (Austin: University of Texas Press, 1976). See also Judith Ismael Bissett, "Consciousness-raising Dramatic Structures in Latin America's Theater of Commitment" (Ph.D. diss., Arizona State University, 1976).

Truman Capote and Norman Mailer have been associated with it, it is questionable whether or not it belongs to the mainstream of current novelistic practice in the United States.[9] By contrast, it would be possible to define Latin American documentary fiction to include many of the novels mentioned above, novels by some of the foremost figures in contemporary Latin American fiction. Certainly, Cortázar's *El libro de Manuel* is a paradigmatic example, with its intercalation of photographically reproduced newspaper clippings in the fictional text. From Oscar Lewis–inspired social ethnographies to the many and varied denunciations of institutional violence in Latin America,[10] documentary narrative is fundamental to Latin American literature.

Rather than merely inventory the many forms such a novelistic modality has assumed in Latin America, in this chapter I will examine in detail five particularly representative examples, plus one—a Brazilian text—that is less characteristic. Significantly, none of these examples makes overt use of documentary materials as does Cortázar's novel or Manuel Puig's footnote-laden *El beso de la mujer araña* (1976), which treats Eros versus civilization in politically and sexually repressive Argentina. And none involves an independently definable fictional component as, again, we have in Cortázar's novel or in the Lukácsian historical novels of David Viñas. By contrast, the five principal titles studied here are based on texts attributed to "real" people: a former black slave in Cuba, students involved in a massacre in Mexico, the victim of a concentration camp in Chile, survivors of a summary political execution in Argentina, and a Colombian sailor lost at sea. What distinguishes these works is not their fundamentally documentary nature (they are routinely classified by libraries as nonfiction). Rather, all are written by important Latin American novelists, all are characterized by a high degree of novelistic "tellability," and, most significant, all involve overtly the problematics of narrating a segment of Latin American reality. As García Márquez notes in

9. Of particular note are the monographic studies by William R. Sibenschuh, *Fictional Techniques and Factual Works*; John Hellmann, *Fables of Fact: The New Journalism as New Fiction*; John Hollowell, *Fact & Fiction: The New Journalism and the Nonfiction Novel*; Mas'ud Zavarzadeh, *The Mythopoeic Reality: The Postwar American Nonfiction Novel*; and Ronald Weber, *The Literature of Fact: Literary Non-Fiction in American Writing*.

10. See the important study of the relationship between violence and art by Ariel Dorfman, *Imaginación y violencia en Améerica*.

the introduction to his documentary narrative *Relato de un náufrago*, which I examine below, "Era tan minucioso y apasionante [el relato compacto y verídico de sus diez días en el mar], que mi único problema literario sería conseguir que el lector lo creyera" ([His compact and true narrative of his ten days at sea] was so detailed and impassioned that my only literary problem would be to get the reader to believe it).[11] It is this foregrounded attention to the relationship between writing and reality, between narrative and fact, between detached novelist and involved participant that creates a special relationship between this form of documentary narrative and the problematics of fiction in Latin America.

II

Originally published in 1957, *Operación masacre* by Rodolfo Walsh (1927-?) is easily the most authentic example of documentary narrative in Latin American fiction.[12] Whereas Julio Cortázar in *El libro de Manuel* (1973) uses actual documents to highlight the fictional narrative,[13] Walsh successfully blends true materials gathered in his investigations with narrative strategies in order to achieve a rhetorically effective presentation of an actual event. Published almost ten years before Truman Capote's much touted "nonfictional novel" *In Cold Blood* (1965), *Operación masacre* anticipates the very techniques presumably developed by the American novelist.

Walsh sets out to re-create the senseless massacre of a group of innocent citizens in the area of La Plata, the capital of the province of Buenos Aires, located about fifty kilometers south of the national capital.[14] In June 1956, a year after Juan Perón was deposed, Peronista military officers stationed at the Campo de Mayo base made an abortive attempt to overthrow the "lib-

11. Gabriel García Márquez, *Relato de un náufrago* . . ., p. 8. Later citations to this work will be made by page number in the text.

12. There are a few adequate studies of Walsh's documentary writings. See, in particular, Aníbal Ford, "Walsh: la reconstrucción de los hechos," in Jorge Lafforgue, ed., *Nueva novela latinoamericana*, 2:272–322. Two other excellent commentaries are Angel Rama, "Rodolfo Walsh: el conflicto de culturas en Argentina," and David Viñas, "Déjenme hablar de Walsh."

13. Concerning the documentary elements in Cortázar's novel, see Marta Morello-Frosch, "La ficción se historifica: Cortázar y Rozenmacher," in *Actas del Simposio Internacional de Estudios Hispánicos* (Budapest: Akadémiai Kiadó, 1978), pp. 401–11.

14. For a fictionalized treatment of these events, see Mario Szichman, *La verdadera crónica falsa* (Buenos Aires: Centro Editor de América Latina, 1972), originally published in 1969 as *Crónica falsa*.

eration" military government. Although this government had claimed that it would operate on the principle of "neither victors nor vanquished," it enacted severe reprisals against Peronista sympathizers, and the massacre Walsh reports involved the summary execution of a group of men taken from a private home where they had putatively gathered to listen to a fight on the radio. The police, claiming that these men were part of the plot to overthrow the government and that they had used the home to store arms, transported them to a field and shot them. Approximately a half-dozen men either escaped in the dark or survived the executioners' volley of shots, and it is on the basis of their story that Walsh pieces together the event. Although some of the men were Peronista sympathizers, there was never a shred of evidence linking them to the unsuccessful attempt to overthrow the anti-Peronista government in power.

Hampered by the problem of identifying and locating the survivors and harassed by a military dictatorship unwilling to admit to such a high-handed fatal mistake, Walsh's story evolved over a ten-year period and appeared in two preliminary versions before the final text was published in 1969. (It is significant that this final version was published by Jorge Alvarez, one of the most dedicated publishers of countercultural materials during the brief period in the late sixties and early seventies when an open diversity of public opinion was permitted in Argentina.)

The prologue to the third and definitive edition of Walsh's narrative provides insights into the problems of investigative reporting in a repressive society, of maintaining an appropriate authorial stance toward one's material, and of distinguishing fact from fiction in a country where reality can outstrip the most creative imagination. Thus, Walsh feels constrained to speak of how he came to discover the first thread that would lead him into the labyrinth of an event with no official reality:

> Seis meses más tarde, una noche asfixiante de verano, frente a un vaso de cerveza, un hombre me dice:
> —Hay un fusilado que vive.
> No sé qué es lo que consigue atraerme en esa historia difusa, lejana, erizada de improbabilidades. No sé por qué pido hablar con ese hombre, por qué estoy hablando con Juan Carlos Livraga.
> Pero después sé. Miro esa cara, el agujero en la mejilla, el agujero más grande en la garganta, la boca quebrada y los ojos opacos don-

de se ha quedado flotando una sombra de muerte. Me siento insultado. . . . Es cosa de reírse, a doce años de distancia, porque se pueden revisar las colecciones de los diarios, y esta historia no existió ni existe.[15]

> (Six months later, one asphyxiating summer evening, seated before a glass of beer, a man says to me:
> "There's someone who has been shot that's alive."
> I don't know what it is about this diffuse and remote story, fraught with impossibilities, that succeeds in attracting me. I don't know why I ask to speak with that man, why I am talking to Juan Carlos Livraga.
> But later I know why. I look into that face, the hole in the cheek, the larger hole in the throat, the broken mouth and the dimmed eyes where a shadow of death remains floating. I feel insulted. . . .
> It's funny because, twelve years later, it is possible to go through the newspaper files, and this story neither existed nor does it exist.)

Divided into three sections, with vignettelike subdivisions ("Los personajes," "Los hechos," "La evidencia"), *Operación* could be read as a seamless piece of fiction. One could even read the prologue, with its highly subjective rhetoric concerning the narrator's commitment to his material, as an integral part of the fictional narrative or as simply one more clever strategy to engage the interest of the reader. In this sense, *Operación* would belong to the *Lord Jim* family of narratives: a singular story, recovered by chance, is interesting for its apparent exotic remoteness from the secure comfort of the reader. Nevertheless, Walsh demands implicitly that his reader recognize the contemporary historical references of his narrative—allusions to the Peronista period and its collapse, to the protagonists of the Revolución Libertadora of 1955, to the abortive uprising at the Campo de Mayo, to subsequent political unrest in the country—and the veracity of claims made about official attempts to thwart such an investigation:

> Era inútil en 1957 pedir justicia para las víctimas de "Operación Masacre." . . . Dentro del sistema, no hay justicia.
> Otros autores vienen trazando una imagen cada vez más finada de esa oligarquía, dominante frente a los argentinos, y dominada frente al extranjero. Que esa clase esté temperamentalmente in-

---

15. Rodolfo Walsh, *Operación masacre*, pp. 11, 13. Further citations will be made by page number in the text.

clinada al asesinato, es una connotación importante que deberá te-
nerse en cuenta cada vez que se encare la lucha contra ella. (p. 195)

(It would have been useless in 1957 to demand justice for the victims of "Operation Massacre." . . . Within the system, there is no
justice.

Other authors have been drawing an ever more final image of that
oligarchy, dominant toward Argentines and dominated in the face
of foreigners. That that class is by temperament inclined toward as-
sassination is an important connotation that must be borne in mind
whenever a struggle against it is undertaken.)

Thus Walsh's narrative, despite its superficial continuities
with a host of modern fictions, demands to be read as a sociohistorical document in which the techniques of fiction, as in
the case of Truman Capote's work several years later, serve to
enhance the texture of truth and the density of human experience. For Rodolfo Walsh, his experience concerns a terrible
and unprovoked act of injustice; it is, however, not an unexplained one, given the contemporary Argentine political reality. What requires explanation, what constitutes the core of
mystery, is not why such an event took place, but rather who
was involved and how that event may be reconstructed in a
convincing fashion. In attempting to reach that goal, the narrator creates an act of revelation for the reader in the act of narrative re-creation.

In this way, *Operación* is based on a structure of reduplication: in reading the narrative creation, the reader repeats the
narrator's discovery of a clandestine event, an event that as far
as official reality is concerned never took place and is nothing
more than a conspiratorial lie—a fiction—propagated to dis-
credit the noble movement of national liberation from the Peronista dictatorship. *Operación* is, therefore, based on a calculated risk: the willingness of the reader to believe the claims of a
highly fictionalized narrative about an unverifiable massacre
rather than the official version that nothing took place. The un-
questionable success of Walsh's book may be based less on the
effectiveness of his narrative talents than on the cooperative
skepticism of a reading public resigned to the mendacity of
official versions. Nevertheless, Walsh's fictionalized strategies
serve as an effective ironic counterpoint to the claim that such a
massacre never happened or that it involved not innocent victims but counterrevolutionary agents. In this sense, Walsh's

"fiction" overtly challenges the "fiction" of the official explanation of the events of mid-1956. Significantly, one of the final sections (35) of the narrative is entitled "La justicia ciega" (Blind Justice). What are some of the fictional techniques utilized by Walsh both to enhance his narrative rhetorically and to juxtapose it ironically to the fabric of official lies? The most obvious is the dramatic reenactment of dialogues among the participants. Walsh's investigation is based on individual interviews of the survivors and other persons implicated in the massacre. Yet it is clear that such dramatic reenactments must be fictional and must constitute the narrator's understanding of the information given him piecemeal by a number of different sources. These narrative re-creations are framed by the narrator's necessarily hypothetical interpretations of the participants' mental states:

> Hay uno por lo menos que se apacigua. Es Troxler. Y al fin ha conseguido que uno de los guardianes lo mire y le sostenga la mirada. Pero hace algo más ese vigilante anónimo. Con la rodilla le da un golpe rápido, deliberado, inequívoco. Una señal.
> Troxler, pues, *ya sabe*. Pero decide jugar una carta audaz, forzar una decisión o por lo menos poner sobre aviso a los otros.
> —¿Qué pasa?—pregunta en voz alta—. ¿Por qué me toca?
> Pánico se refleja en la mirada del policía. Ya está arrepentido de lo que hizo. El cabo lo mira con suspicacia.
> —Por nada, señor—contesta atropelladamente—. Fue sin querer. (pp. 92–93)

> (There is one at least who calms down. It's Troxler. And he has succeeded at last in getting one of the guards to look at him and to hold his gaze. But that anonymous guard does something more. With his knee he gives him a rapid, deliberate, unmistakable blow. A sign.
> Troxler, thus, *now knows*. But he decides to play a daring card, to force a decision or at least to put the others on guard.
> "What's going on?" he asks out loud. "Why have you touched me?"
> Panic shows in the policeman's face. He is already sorry he did it. The corporal looks at him askance.
> "No reason, sir," he answers clumsily. "It was an accident.")

The second novelistic strategy, one associated with modern fiction, is the "mosaic narrative." Rather than relating events in a strictly chronological order, the narrative in the first section of *Operación* presents the protagonists. The second section summarizes the event, moving with the leisure of a psychological novel among the consciousnesses of the participants. In the concluding segment, the judicial treatment of the case is analyzed with the goal of belying the government's self-serving explanations. Thus, the action of the story is set aside in favor of exploring the complex reactions of individuals involved in an irrational historical process that they only vaguely understand although they are its sacrificial victims (see p. 70).

The following segment is typical of Walsh's use of documentary information gathered from the participants, psychological speculation, and dramatic re-creation:

> Ya casi ha terminado de cenar Francisco Garibotti—un bife con huevos fritos comió esa noche—cuando llaman a la puerta.
> Es don Carranza.
> —Vino a sacármelo. Para que me lo devolvieran muerto—recordará Florinda Allende con rencor en la voz. (pp. 28–29)

> (Francisco Garibotti has almost finished eating—steak with fried eggs is what he ate that evening—when someone comes to the door.
> It's Don Carranza.
> What can Nicolás Carranza want?
> "He came to take him away from me. So I would get him back dead," Florinda Allende was to recall with bitterness in her voice.)

The unannounced transition from the pluperfect arrival of Nicolás Carranza, to the present rhetorical question posed to the reader, and then to the "future past" reply given by Garibotti's wife when the investigative reporter asks her the same question is an outstanding example of Walsh's very effective narrative strategies. By contrast with the rather flat autobiographical narrative of *Biografía de un cimarrón* (see section VI below), the unhighlighted reporting of *La noche de Tlatelolco* (see section III below), or the explicit disjunction of fiction and document in *El libro de Manuel*, the narrative texture of *Operación* is particularly novelistic in blending into a single discourse the disparate elements of narrative speculation and authentic quotation.

Yet another novelistic device is a form of narrative withholding characteristic of detective fiction. Along with the overt references to unknown elements (the final section of the first part is entitled "Las incógnitas" [Unknown Elements]), to what "we will never know," Walsh effects a suspenseful rhythm in his narrative by withholding information at certain points and by shifting focus from one person to another or from one circumstance to another. Although the general outline of events has been given in the prologue, by momentarily defying the reader's natural desire to have an explanation in full at any one point in the narrator's exposition, *Operación* makes use of one of the hoariest techniques of the storyteller's art:

> En el inextricable italiano del viejo sereno se destaca una palabra, martillada a intervalos regulares "revoluzion. . .revoluzion.". . . Dos súbitos guardias armados con carabina imponen silencio desde la puerta. En todo el vasto edificio se ha producido un cambio apenas perceptible, pero siniestro. La actitud antes despreocupada de los vigilantes se torna hosca, ceñuda. Voces, repiquetear de pasos en la galería de la comisaría adquieren singulares resonancias. Después, prolongados silencios.
>
> Ajeno a todo, desparramado sobre un banco, como un gran Neptuno negro, el sargento Díaz ronca estertorosamente. Su amplio tórax asciende y desciende con pausado ritmo. El sueño le barniza el rostro con una máscara impasible.
>
> Los demás empiezan a mirarlo con fastidio, con espanto. (p. 79; these are the final paragraphs of one of the sections)

> (In the inextricable Italian of the old night watchman one word stands out, hammered at regular intervals "revoluzion . . . revoluzion." . . .
>
> Two sudden guards armed with carbines impose silence from the door. In the whole vast building a scarcely perceptible but sinister change has taken place. The previously unconcerned attitude of the guards has become sullen and grim. Voices, footfalls in the hallways of the police station take on singular resonances, followed by prolonged silences.
>
> Alien to it all, sprawled out on a bench like a black Neptune, Sergeant Díaz snores noisily. His broad chest rises and falls rhythmically. Sleep burnishes his face with an impassive mask.
>
> The others begin to watch him disgustedly, fearfully.)

By playing on the parallel between the reader's desire to know and the participants' inability to explain the tragic circumstances in which they are caught and on the homology between the narrator's and the reader's discovery of a nefarious event, Walsh constructs perhaps the most sophisticated example of Latin American documentary narrative in the service of sociopolitical awareness. The narrator's cry of frustration in the face of too much reality anticipates that of readers unable to withstand the onslaught of a truth they are virtually helpless to repeal:

Después no quiero recordar más, ni la voz del locutor en la madrugada anunciando que dieciocho civiles han sido ejecutados en Lanús, ni la ola de sangre que anega al país hasta la muerte de Valle [a counterrevolutionary]. Tengo demasiado para una sola noche. Valle no me interesa. Perón no me interesa, la revolución no me interesa. ¿Puedo volver al ajedrez? (p. 10)

(Later I want to recall nothing more, not the voice of the announcer informing us at dawn that eighteen civilians have been executed in Lanús, not the wave of blood that washes over the country until the death of Valle. I have had enough for one night. Valle does not interest me. Perón does not interest me, the revolution does not interest me. May I return to my chess?)

III

If the Viet Nam War marked a loss of innocence for the United States, the events surrounding the massacre of students by police at Tlatelolco, or the Plaza de las Tres Culturas, on the night of 2 October 1968 had a similar impact on Mexico's self-image. Whereas the citizen of the United States had to recognize that an American military involvement might be base and self-serving rather than noble, the shooting of students exercising their legal and constitutional right of assembly brought to the attention of the Mexican public an ugly truth: despite Mexico's tradition of stable government under the strong "guided democracy" of the ruling PRI (Institutional Revolutionary party), repression of civil liberties and human rights could assume the same terrible proportions in Mexico as in Argentina or Paraguay.

A number of elements contributed to the tremendous psychological impact of the Tlatelolco incident. The massacre followed a series of student protest movements that spanned the summer months and early fall. It occurred when a large array of foreign correspondents (including Oriana Fallaci) and tourists were in Mexico for the Olympic games. To the students and their supporters, it proved that the government of Gustavo Díaz Ordaz and the ruling oligarchy supporting him were not going to tolerate serious dissent.[16]

16. The following are a sample of works on Tlatelolco: Sócrates A. Campos Lemus, *El otoño de revolución (octubre)* (Mexico City: B. Costa-Amic, 1973); Juan Miguel de Mora, *Tlatelolco, por fin toda la verdad*, 7th ed. (Mexico City: Asociados, 1975); and Javier Barros Sierra, *1968: conversaciones con Gastón García Cantú* (Mexico City: Siglo XXI, 1972).

Indeed, Tlatelolco has acquired such a profound meaning in contemporary Mexican culture that it has been the subject of a book-length essay by Octavio Paz and has inspired virtually a subgenre of recent Mexican literature.[17] *La noche de Tlatelolco* (1971) by Elena Poniatowska (1933–) is the only documentary narrative besides Cortázar's *El libro de Manuel* and Barnet's *Biografía de un cimarrón* that has been translated into English. It is the most documentary of the texts studied in this essay and, consequently, the least "novelistic" if viewed in terms of fictional elements or devices.[18] Nevertheless, it is novelistic in the sense that it sustains a complex narrative structure. And, although *Noche* has a place in a bibliography of contemporary social history, it is frequently read as a contribution to the contemporary Latin American novel. To read *Noche* as more novel than document does not detract from its quality as documentary testimonial. Rather—as is true for all recent documentary and historical fiction in Latin America—such a reading testifies to the continuity in that culture of fiction and reality and the importance of productive "mythic" factuality.[19]

The nearly three hundred pages of *Noche* are divided into two roughly equal sections, "Ganar la calle" and "La noche de Tlatelolco." The first part refers to the various student demonstrations and skirmishes with police during the summer of 1968 and the second to the confrontation on 2 October, in which the

17. Octavio Paz, *Posdata* (Mexico City: Siglo XXI, 1970). Published in English as *The Other Mexico: Critique of the Pyramid*, trans. Lysander Kemp (New York: Grove Press, 1972). Significantly, the first chapter is entitled "Olimpiada y Tlatelolco." See also Luis Leal, "Tlatelolco, Tlatelolco," and Jean Franco, "The Critique of the Pyramid and Mexican Narrative after 1968," in Rose S. Minc, ed., *Latin American Fiction Today: A Symposium*, pp. 49–60.

18. There has been little criticism on Poniatowska beyond brief notes and reviews. See Beth Miller and Alfonso González, "Elena Poniatowska," in their *26 autoras del México actual*, pp. 299–321. Poniatowska speaks of *Noche* in "Un libro que me fue dado"; also included in the same issue of *Vida literaria* as Poniatowska's article are commentaries by other writers. See also Dolly J. Young and William D. Young, "The New Journalism in Mexico: Two Women Writers [Poniatowska and María Luisa Mendoza]"; Elizabeth Starčević, "Elena Poniatowska: Witness for the People," in *Contemporary Women Authors of Latin America*, pp. 72–77; Monica Flori, "El mundo femenino de Marta Lynch y Elena Poniatowska"; and Lucía Fox-Lockert, "Elena Poniatowska," in her *Women Novelists of Spain and Spanish America*, pp. 260–77.

19. One can only make such summary statements at great critical risk. Clearly, this is the understanding of Carpentier's *lo real-maravilloso* and of Carlos Fuentes's view of the contemporary Spanish American novel in *La nueva novela hispanoamericana*, in direct contrast to the "anamythopoesis" of hard-line Marxists like Hernán Vidal, *Literatura hispanoamericana e ideología liberal: surgimiento y crisis (una problemática sobre la dependencia en torno a la narrativa del boom)*.

police, apparently obeying orders to end the protest activities, opened fire on the unarmed students. But there is no clear break between the two sections, and the development of the material is chronological in only a very general fashion. It is evident that Poniatowska means to relate the two phases of the 1968 events as more than simply a sequence of escalating violence. While it is apparent that the relationship between the protest movement and Mexico's hosting of the Olympic games was no accident, both the author and her interviewees maintain that the movement developed out of natural causes and not from an effort to embarrass the government in its sponsorship of the games (the importance to Mexico of being the first Latin American country to host the games is obvious; to a great degree it was meant to signify Mexico's mature, international stature).

Rather, Poniatowska and the students—as well as the teachers, intellectuals, and members of the general public whom she interviewed—insist that there had emerged in Mexico a general pattern of repression of dissent. The Díaz Ordaz government, either cynically or stupidly, seemed determined to exercise the dictatorial control associated with military regimes in Latin America and not with the sort of functioning democracy Mexico claimed to be. Moreover, the fact that the 2 October massacre took place in the Plaza de las Tres Culturas has been interpreted as symbolic of Mexico's ties to the blood sacrifices of its Aztec roots.

But Poniatowska only suggests this latter interpretation; it was left to writers like Octavio Paz and Carlos Fuentes to provide adequate literary elaboration.[20] Instead, Poniatowska's handling of the material is strictly documentary. The texture of *Noche* is provided by the skillful weaving together of fragments, usually a few lines to half a page in length, although occasionally longer, based on interviews she conducted with participants and bystanders: many members of both groups were still incarcerated over a year later when she was working on the manuscript.[21] These fragments are punctuated with slogans

20. See Fuentes's play *Todos los gatos son pardos* (1970), which ends by viewing the massacre at Tlatelolco in the context of the Mexican-Aztec-Christian-postrevolutionary sacrificial culture.
21. The only specific observations on the structure of *Noche* are those of Ronald Christ in "The Author as Editor."

taken from the banners and signs carried by the students, as well as with material from various other documentary sources, such as newspaper reports and official declarations. Finally, on a very few occasions, Poniatowska intervenes to offer her own personal point of view. Otherwise, with the exception of statements in the interviews addressed to her by name, the authorial presence is limited to the not insignificant ordering of the material that we read.[22]

Although Poniatowska includes material from officials and citizens who attribute seditious and immoral objectives to the students, the overall tone of *Noche* creates the sense of a tragic event that transcended the will of the participants to control it. It is in this sense that the massacre at Tlatelolco was neither an isolated "accident" nor the folly of a particular dictatorial ambition, but rather a dramatic example of the repression inherent in the Mexican system of government. The following is one of Poniatowska's rare explicit interventions in her documentary report:

> En su mayoría estos testimonios fueron recogidos en octubre y noviembre de 1968. Los estudiantes presos dieron los suyos en el curso de los dos años siguientes. Este relato les pertenece. Está hecho con sus palabras, sus luchas, sus errores, su dolor y su asombro. Aparecen también sus "aceleradas", su ingenuidad, su confianza. Sobre todo les agradezco a las madres, a los que perdieron al hijo, al hermano, el haber accedido a hablar. El dolor es un acto absolutamente solitario. Hablar de él resulta casi intolerable; indagar, horadar, tiene sabor de insolencia.
>
> Este relato recuerda a una madre que durante días permaneció quieta, endurecida bajo el golpe y, de repente, como animal herido—un animal a quien le extraen las entrañas—dejó salir del centro de su vida, de la vida misma que ella había dado, un ronco, un desgarrado grito. Un grito que daba miedo, miedo por el mal absoluto que se le puede hacer a un ser humano; ese grito distorsionado que todo lo rompe, el ay de la herida definitiva, la que no podrá cicatrizar jamás, la de la muerte del hijo.
>
> Aquí está todo el eco del grito de los que murieron y el grito de los que quedaron. Aquí está su indagación y su protesta. Es el grito mudo que se atoró en miles de gargantas, en miles de ojos desor-

---

22. Poniatowska's narrative is dedicated to her brother Jan, who died at Tlatelolco. Except for a few quotes, however, this personal relationship is virtually silenced.

bitados por el espanto el 2 de octubre de 1968, en la noche de Tlatelolco.[23]

(The majority of the following interviews were recorded in October and November 1968. The students who had been imprisoned offered their testimony during the two years following Tlatelolco. This is their story, woven out of their words, their struggles, their mistakes, their pain, and their bewilderment at the turn events took. Their impatience, their ingenuousness, their confidence also play a part in it. I am especially grateful to mothers who lost their sons and daughters, to brothers and sisters of the dead who were kind enough to allow me to record their words. Grief is a very personal thing. Putting it into words is almost unbearable; hence asking questions, digging for facts, borders on an invasion of people's privacy.

This story is also that of a mother so stunned that for days and days she uttered scarcely a word, and then suddenly, like a wounded animal—an animal whose belly is being ripped apart—she let out a hoarse, heart-rending cry, from the very center of her life, from the very life that had been taken from her. A terrible cry, a cry of terror at the utter evil that can befall a human being; the sort of wild keening that is the end of everything, the wail of ultimate pain from the wound that will never heal, the death of a son.

In these pages there echo the cries of those who died and the cries of those who lived on after them. These pages express their outrage and their protest: the mute cry that stuck in thousands of throats, the blind grief in thousands of horror-stricken eyes on October 2, 1968, the night of Tlatelolco.) (p. 199)

If Rodolfo Walsh's *Operación masacre* depends for its impact on the willingness of the reader to believe that savage torture and illegal executions are integral to Argentine life, the power of Poniatowska's narrative derives from the incredulity of the reader, mirrored in the statements of the individuals Poniatowska interviewed, that such events could happen in Mexico, a country that in the twentieth century has claimed to be above the human-rights violations characteristic of Latin America. When Poniatowska includes material referring to the arbitrary behavior of the police toward students and bystanders, the disappearance of individuals whisked away in broad daylight in unmarked cars, the refusal of authorities to answer inquiries

---

23. Elena Poniatowska, *La noche de Tlatelolco: testimonios de historia oral*, 8th ed., p. 164. Further citations will be made by page number in the text. *Noche* was published in English as *Massacre in Mexico*, trans. Helen R. Lane; the translations included herein are from this edition.

concerning the arrested or the detained, the excessive sentences imposed in violation of accepted legal principles, the torture sessions at police headquarters, and, finally, the explosion of violence by a government against its own citizens at Tlatelolco, she challenges the sacred myths of modern Mexico. Her publisher's difficulty in keeping the book in print when it appeared in 1971 testifies to the fact that there were readers willing to risk the challenge to their incredulity:

Cuando me di cuenta de que el helicóptero bajaba peligrosamente sobre la Plaza de la Tres Culturas y ametrallaba a la gente—se veían rayas grises en el cielo—me quedé tan asombrada que dije: "No, esto no es verdad, es una película, esto sólo lo he visto en el cine. ¡No son balas de verdad!" Seguí caminando, como ida, como loca hasta que la gente me detuvo.

*Elvira B. de Concheiro, madre de familia (p. 174)

(When I realized that the helicopter had come down dangerously low, circling right above the heads of the crowd in the Plaza de las Tres Culturas and firing on everybody—we could see the gray streaks of tracer bullets in the sky—I was so dumbfounded I said to myself, I can't believe it—it's like in a movie! I've never seen anything like this except in the movies. Those just can't be real bullets! I wandered around in a daze, as though I'd gone out of my mind, until finally somebody grabbed me by the arm and stopped me.) (pp. 211–12)

These features lead us to consider the narrative aspects of *Noche* and its place, as documentary, among contemporary Latin American novels. A conventional novel like Carlos Fuentes's *La cabeza de la hidra* treats a fictional circumstance as though it were real: *Cabeza* is the first Mexican espionage novel by a major writer, and it deals with American, Israeli, and Arab intrigue over Mexico's huge petroleum industry. Poniatowska's documentary, on the other hand, deals with a real event so monumental and terrible in its implications that it challenges the credulity of participants, witnesses, and, in the final instance, the readers of her text (indeed, there must be otherwise intelligent Mexicans who doubt that the massacre at Tlatelolco took place). Thus, the author's goal is not to present an "academic" analysis of a particular moment in recent Mexican history but to re-create the sense and the feel of an event in order to highlight its inescapable reality.

From a novelist's point of view, Poniatowska eschews the procedure of serializing a number of individual and discrete interviews—the strategy popularized by Oscar Lewis in his oral anthropological research—in favor of the mosaic patterning so characteristic of contemporary fiction. That is to say, although she interviewed a specific number of individuals, the words of no one of the principal interviewees are given as a block. Rather, the text of *Noche* moves back and forth among a basic cast of speakers, and it would be necessary to gather quotes spread over the full extent of *Noche* to recover the testimony given by a specific person. Instead, the declarations of each individual (and it is reasonable to suppose that some persons were interviewed in one session, others in several) are fragmented in order to provide clusters of comments on significant topics: police brutality, the causes of the movement, the role of students, the reactions of bystanders, the attitudes of teachers and administrators toward the protest movement, and so on. For example, one section deals with participants' emotional reactions to memories of Tlatelolco:

> Me gusta octubre; es el mes del año que más me gusta. El aire es tan transparente que la ciudad se arrellana como en una cuna de montañas, las calles desembocan en los volcanes morados, azul oscuro, afelpado de pronto—como si pudiera yo extender la mano, tocarlos y mi mano se hundiera en lomos aborregados, tibios, calientes bajo el sol de octubre; un sol que todavía calienta. . .Desde aquí [la prisión Lecumberri] no se ve nada, sólo barrotes verdes con las púas que regresan hacia nosotros, sólo la lámina verde de las celdas cerradas. Pero huele a octubre, sabe a octubre—ahora en 1969—, y trato de pensar que este octubre nuevo se llevó al de 68, antes de que todos muriéramos—porque nosotros también morimos un poco—en la Plaza de las Tres Culturas.
>
> *Ernesto Olvera, profesor de Matemáticas de la Preparatoria 1 de la UNAM (p. 152)

(I really like October—it's my favorite month of the year. The air is so clear then that it's as though the city were lolling in the cradle of mountains around it; you look down the streets and there the volcanoes are, a dark, velvety blue all of a sudden—it always seems as though I could reach out and touch them, and my hand would sink into the soft fleece on their sides, basking in the October sunshine, still nice and warm. . . . You can't see anything from in here, just iron bars painted green with spikes pointing toward you, just the green sheet-metal doors of the cells that are shut up tight. But it smells of October in the air, it tastes of October now, in the year 1969—and I try to pretend that October this year is just like October of '68, before we all died—because all of us died a little there in the Plaza de las Tres Culturas.) (pp. 159–60)

It could be argued that such a textual strategy is paradigmatically documentary and thus antithetical to fictional narrative. After all, historical novels, while they may seek to re-create an era or an event, focus on the internal coherence and identity of specific individuals; even documentary novels like Capote's *In Cold Blood* strive for a sense of the feelings and motivations of concrete individuals. By contrast, Poniatowska's use of her interview material makes it difficult to derive a sense of any one of the participants, with the possible exception of two or three whose words recur with special insistence. Nevertheless, *Noche*, in repudiating the need to portray individual "psychologies," is in the mainstream of contemporary fiction, especially the new Latin American novel. Juan Rulfo's *Pedro Páramo* (1955), Julio Cortázar's *Rayuela* (1963), Carlos Fuentes's *La región más transparente* (1958), Manuel Puig's *La traición de Rita Hayworth* (1968), Severo Sarduy's *De donde son los cantantes* (1967), and Mario Vargas Llosa's *La ciudad y los perros* (1963) are all novels based on narrative and "psychological" fragmentation, in which discrete individuals and events must be pieced together. Vargas Llosa's *La casa verde* (1966) is perhaps the most famous example of such an *écriture*: in it individuals have different names as they participate in different but homologous situations. Thus, *Noche* is an excellent example of the nonpsychological or "nonpersonalist" novel that Noé Jitrik has described as typical of contemporary fiction in his *El no existente caballero*,[24] and parallels with American and international fiction—John Barth or Donald Barthelme, for example—should be obvious.

In this sense, one cannot speak of *Noche* as more "authentic" or "real" because of its overt use of interview materials and the fragmentation that impedes the sense of "round characters," to use E. M. Forster's famous term. Rather, the ironic framing— the foregone conclusion of the event as the point of departure for the chain of occurrences represented—the authorial intervention in organizing the material gathered, the eloquent juxtaposition of oral texts with various other sources, the interplay between personal commentaries and impersonal, antiphonic choruses like the banners and posters are all conscious artistic decisions that lend *Noche* its special narrative and novelistic texture.

24. Noé Jitrik, *El no existente caballero: la idea de personaje y su evolución en la narrativa latinoamericana.* See also Fuentes, *La nueva novela*, pp. 16–23.

IV

It would perhaps be an error to associate documentary narrative with unusually dramatic events in the sociopolitical life of a society: institutional violence is such an integral part of Latin America that it is difficult to avoid the conclusion that its appearance in Latin American literature has been predominantly documentary rather than fictional since the time of independence and the first sense of the loss of ideals and guiding myths.

Nevertheless, events like the Tlatelolco massacre in Mexico City or the military coup in Chile in 1973 have been perceived as major advances in the contest between democratic ideals and official repression. It is therefore not surprising that the inevitable fictional treatments are complemented by documentary narratives responding to the urgency of "reality" with the symbolic power of literature. We have seen how Poniatowska's narrative of the Tlatelolco massacre is predicated on the strategy of disbelief. In opposition to the cliché that fiction asks us to believe in the reality of an imaginary narrative space, Poniatowska takes a historically definable context and demands that we believe that the incredible can occur. Juan Rulfo asks us to believe that in the fictional realm of *Pedro Páramo* the dead continue the discourse of life; in *La noche de Tlatelolco*, Poniatowska asks us to believe that official repression has reached such a point in Mexico that the incredible may take place: innocent citizens, exercising the constitutional rights of assembly and free expression, may be massacred by a cynical government.

The military takeover in Chile on 11 September 1973 engendered a truly impressive body of literature: virtually every Chilean writer of note has attempted to render an adequate portrayal of the Allende phenomenon and the coup. The Unión Popular government triggered not only one of the most vicious military coups in recent Latin American history but also a tragic loss of national innocence, a realization of just how fragile the much-touted Chilean liberal and democratic tradition was.[25] Narrative treatments range from the highly allegorical

25. Consult the collection of texts by important Chilean authors in Antonio Skármeta, ed., *Joven narrativa chilena después del golpe* (Clear Creek, Ind.: The American Hispanist, 1976). In addition to Skármeta's introduction, see also the notes and articles in *Literatura chilena en el exilio* (Hollywood, 1977–), and the "Coloquio sobre literatura chilena en la resistencia y en el exilio," *Casa de las Américas* 112 (1979):73–109.

version by Chile's major novelist, José Donoso, *Casa de campo* (1978), to the barely controlled denunciations like Fernando Alegría's *Paso de los gansos* (1975) or Antonio Skármeta's *Soñé que la nieve ardía* (1975). In a documentary vein, Enrique Lafourcade's *Salvador Allende* (1973) and Hernán Valdés's *Tejas Verdes* (1974) are two of the best examples. Lafourcade weaves together explicitly documentary material with a necessarily fictional evocation of Allende's stream-of-consciousness ramblings on his government and its fate. The structural strategy of *Salvador Allende* is reminiscent of the conjunction of documentary materials and fictional narrative in Cortázar's *El libro de Manuel*, and in the representation of Allende's preverbal consciousness it bears affinities with Roa Bastos's *Yo el Supremo*. However, because its portrayal of the complexities of the Allende phenomenon is not particularly convincing, Lafourcade's work has never achieved recognition as an important post-1973 Chilean narrative.

Hernán Valdés (1943–) is one of the most important of the writers of the Allende period. His *Tejas Verdes* (1974), subtitled *Diario de un campo de concentración en Chile*, re-creates the time he spent in the Tejas Verdes camp near the port of San Antonio after the 1973 coup.[26] Valdés was a prisoner a little over a month, during which time he was subjected to the torture and generally degrading and brutal treatment associated with such institutions in modern Latin America. As such, *Tejas Verdes* belongs to an extensive bibliography of fictional and documentary materials that treat the violence of repressive Latin American societies. These materials focus on the use of torture, secret police, extra-legal death squads, and clandestine jails as institutionalized means of social and political control. From Eduardo Pavlovsky's drama on professional torturers, *El señor Galíndez* (1973), and novels on official torture like Manuel Puig's *El beso de la mujer araña* (1976) or Carlos Martínez Moreno's *El color que el infierno nos escondiera* (1981), to the personal testimony by Jacobo Timerman, *Prisoner without a Name, Cell without a Number* (1980), there is a constellation of works in which it is difficult, and probably fruitless, to attempt to distinguish between the fictional and the documentary.

26. It is noteworthy that Valdés contributed a segment of *Tejas Verdes* to Skármeta's *Joven narrativa chilena*. Juan Armando Epple discusses *Tejas Verdes* in the context of concentration-camp literature in Chile: "Esa literatura que surge de un cerco de púas." Kenneth W. Massey comments on Valdés's text in "From behind the Bars of Signifiers and Signifieds."

What is unique about *Tejas Verdes* is not the voice it adds to the tragic chorus demanding recognition of human rights in Latin America: it would be impossible to provide a hierarchy for these voices, each powerfully eloquent in its own fashion. What is singular about Valdés's narrative is the conjunction of the unquestionably true statements regarding his personal experiences in the Tejas Verdes camp with his use of a fundamentally hypothetical diary in order to portray those experiences. The diary format, particularly when used to transmit alleged fact, presupposes that the narrator/author has the opportunity to transcribe events on a day-by-day basis, in moments of recollection and reflection. Purportedly, such a document possesses the spontaneity of the moment and the accuracy provided by immediate recounting. In contrast to chronological memoirs, which use the past tense to describe events, the diary uses the present tense to convey the continuity between an event and its prompt commitment to paper.

Valdés divides his diary into thirty-one dated segments, one for each day of his detention, and his narrative is written in the present tense. However, he recognizes in his preface that, since he was actually unable to maintain a diary during his stay at Tejas Verdes, what he presents is a legitimate re-creation of what he would have written had he been able:

> *El lector tiene ante sí el diario de un prisionero en uno de los sectores del campo de concentración militar de Tejas Verdes, situado a pocos kilómetros del puerto de San Antonio, en la provincia de Santiago. Evidentemente, se trata de un diario reconstituido (nadie puede concebir licencias como las de redactar y guardar ningún tipo de texto en esas condiciones), pero en este proceso de reconstitución he hecho todo lo posible por conservar la más fidedigna cronología de la cotidianidad, lo que resulta harto difícil si se tiene en cuenta la total ausencia de referencias y plazos temporales que caracteriza a estos lugares.*[27]

> [*The reader has before him the diary of a prisoner in one of the sectors of the military concentration camp of Tejas Verdes, located a few kilometers from the port of San Antonio, in the province of Santiago. It is evident that it is a reconstructed diary (no one could conceive of the privilege of writing and keeping any text in conditions such as these), but in this process of reconstruction I have done everything possible to maintain the most faithful chronology of daily events, something that is quite difficult if you keep in*

27. Hernán Valdés, *Tejas Verdes, diario de un campo de concentración en Chile*, p. 5. Further citations will be given in the text.

mind the complete lack of points of reference and time frames characteristic of such places.]

While prisoners characteristically lose their sense of time and identity when subjected to the unremitting brutality of physical abuse in places like Tejas Verdes, the relative brevity of Valdés's internment lends credibility to his day-by-day re-creation of events. The "Nota preliminar" is dated May 1974, and the last entry in the diary is dated 15 March 1974; this proximity of dates serves to validate Valdés's claims to accuracy.

Such a combination of circumstances testifies, of course, to Valdés's determination to bear personal witness to the terrible violation of human rights in Chile. His testimony is synecdochal of that of the thousands who have died in places like Tejas Verdes or who have remained silent rather than risk further persecution. Although Valdés speaks out for many from the safety of Barcelona, the juxtaposition of the restrictions of the concentration camp with the hypothetical re-creation of the diary acquires, in terms of narrative discourse, a special meaning. The diary entitled *Tejas Verdes*, with its credibly accurate re-creation of life inside the concentration camp, emerges as an ex post facto defiance of the silence and the loss of personal identity through verbal expression imposed by the extralegal prison system.

There is ample evidence that strict silence is used as a strategy to destroy political prisoners, and the eloquence of the fictive day-by-day entries in Valdés's diary serves as a defiant counterpoint to the real, Draconian circumscriptions of imprisonment. In contrast, the only legitimate forms of communication become the demands for information imposed by the torture and interrogation sessions:

—¿Y esta carta, huevón? ¿De qué libro habla, qué es esto de que va a caer Nixon?

Recuerdo que es la carta de un amigo norteamericano, que me cuenta que está traduciendo una novela mía al inglés, y que al final me expresa su satisfacción por la caída inminente de Nixon. Lo explico. De pronto me doy cuenta de que el terror me ha hecho olvidar el terror fundamental: que hubieran descubierto mis artículos. En alguna región muy distante, entre las dudas, siento un cierto alivio.

—¿De qué trata tu novela?

La pregunta me desconcierta más que cualquier otra. Mi memoria queda bloqueada, en blanco. Cada vez que alguien, antes, me ha hecho una pregunta semejante, también me he sentido incapaz de responder pero era otra cosa. Ahora tengo que hablar, los alientos están encima de mi cara, los puños están impacientes. (p. 39)

("And this letter, asshole? What book does it mean, what's this about Nixon being about to fall?"

I remember that it's a letter from a friend in the United States who tells me that he is translating one of my novels into English and that toward the end he expresses to me his satisfaction over Nixon's imminent fall. I explain this. Suddenly I realize that terror has made me forget the basic fear: that they may have discovered my articles. In some distant region, among doubts, I feel a certain relief.

"What's your novel about?"

The question catches me off-guard more than any other. My memory becomes blocked, a blank. Before, whenever anyone has asked me such a question, I have also felt unable to respond, but that was something else. Now I must answer, their breath is on my face, their fists are impatient.)

The proscriptions against expression versus the demands for information, the imaginary worlds of the novelist versus the all-too-real world of a particular political process, the semi-consciousness of the brutalized prisoner versus the eloquence of a personal testimony, the unreality of the experience of the moment versus the painfully vivid recall of a subsequent reflection: these are some of the juxtapositions Valdés's document makes use of in order to highlight the uniqueness of its narrative:

Hablar desde aquí [Barcelona] de todo eso como de una realidad esfumada, como de una situación histórica única dilapidada por el temor, suena a pesadilla; pero más todavía reconocernos a nosotros mismos, en la medida en que hablamos, como sobrevivientes de esa realidad. Porque, si logramos salir de aquí alguna vez ¿qué seremos si no? En el mejor caso, individuos aislados, ocupándonos oscuramente de mantener nuestras vidas. Melancólicos de lo que no supimos hacer con la historia. (p. 72)

(To talk about all this from here as though talking about a fuzzy reality, a unique historical situation decayed by terror, sounds like a nightmare. But even more so to recognize ourselves, as we talk, as survivors of that reality. Because if we are successful in finally getting out of here, what else will we be but survivors? The best we can expect is to be isolated individuals, obscurely concerned with sustaining our lives, melancholic about what we were incapable of doing with history.)

The deictic *aquí* of this passage, in the context of the diary's defiance of the restrictions against personal expression in the concentration camp, assumes an ironic function. As a reference to the locus of Valdés the prisoner, it alludes to the problem of continuity between the "situación histórica" of the narrator and of his colleagues and their imprisonment in Tejas Verdes: their personal suffering is not an isolated circumstance but an integral part of an ideological process to which they bear symbolic witness. It is only in this way that the political prisoners can struggle against the psychological destruction sought by their jailers.

But as the point of reference of Valdés the memorialist—the writer who allows himself the license of creating the diary he would like to have been able to maintain during his incarceration—*aquí* alludes to the problem of creating continuity between the timeless and nebulous domain of miserable suffering and the commitment to bear witness felt by the individual ten thousand miles removed from Tejas Verdes. Valdés disavows any literary pretensions for his document (*literary* surely means here "decorative style" and not symbolic power), while speaking of the challenge of reality to the Chilean writer:

> *Estas páginas están escritas a toda prisa, "al calor de la memoria". Por lo mismo, no debe buscarse en ellas ningún tipo de elaboración literaria. El lenguaje es fundamentalmente funcional y esto ha significado para mí una experiencia nueva. Agradecimientos aparte, la Junta militar, al barrer con el mito de la democracia chilena y al implantar en la vida real un fascismo que sólo conocíamos por referencias culturales, nos ha propuesto un abundante material de inspiración concreta a los escritores que en Chile no sabíamos qué hacer con nuestra inaprensible y contradictoria realidad. Este libro no es sino un borrador de lo que serán sus productos. (p. 6)*

> (*These pages have been written hastily, "under the heat of memory." As a consequence, one should not seek in them any sort of literary elaboration. Their language is essentially functional, and this has meant a new experience for me. Expressions of gratitude aside, the military Junta, by sweeping away the myth of Chilean democracy and by imposing on a real life a fascism that we only knew about from cultural references, has provided us writers with abundant material of concrete inspiration, writers in Chile who had no idea of what we were going to do with our elusive and contradictory reality. This book is nothing more than the rough draft of what those products will be.*)

The artful strategy of interplaying silence and expressiveness—a strategy that is literary in a sense acceptable to a novelist of Valdés's qualifications—lends *Tejas Verdes* a power as documentary narrative quite beyond its validity as a source of sociohistorical information, frustrating the goal of the oppressors: "Se estima que una persona que pase por los campos implicará por lo menos la despolitización de una familia. En un par de años o antes se habrá logrado el milagro de un país de sordomudos" (The idea is that a person who passes through the camps represents at least the depolitization of one family. Within a few years, if not before, the miracle of a country of deaf-mutes will have been achieved; p. 6). Thus, *Tejas Verdes* stands as a superb example of Latin American documentary narrative precisely because of its defiance of the primacy of collective silence.

V

While the most renowned Latin American writers may be associated with the broad genre of "testimonial literature"—literature that in varying degrees fictionalizes and allegorizes recognizable individuals and events in Latin American society and politics—relatively few have written specifically documentary narratives. *Relato de un náufrago que estuvo diez días a la deriva en una balsa sin comer ni beber, que fue proclamado héroe de la patria, besado por las reinas de la belleza y hecho rico por la publicidad, y luego aborrecido por el gobierno y olvidado para siempre* (1970), by Gabriel García Márquez (1928–), is a significant exception.[28] Published in 1955 as a series of newspaper articles in Bogotá's *El Espectador*, *Relato* would never have been reprinted in book form had not the young reporter gone on to become one of Latin America's most famous novelists. Indeed, García Márquez observes in his introductory note that he was persuaded to allow publication of *Relato* only because publication would permit him to turn the royalties over to the work's true author, the forgotten seaman of the Colombian naval destroyer *Caldas*. But *Relato* only functions as documentary narrative in the

28. Despite the importance of García Márquez's writings, *Relato* has received only brief comments: Klaus Müller-Bergh, "*Relato de un náufrago*: Gabriel García Márquez's Tale of Shipwreck and Survival at Sea"; and Jorge Ruffinelli, "Diez días en el mar," in Pedro Simón Martínez, ed., *Sobre García Márquez*, pp. 207–9. See also Ruffinelli's "Un periodista llamado Gabriel García Márquez," in his *Crítica en marcha, ensayos sobre literatura latinoamericana*, pp. 56–59. The standard monographic study, by novelist Mario Vargas Llosa, *García Márquez: historia de un deicidio*, does not consider *Relato*.

context of its republication. The seaman's narrative is not much more than a detailed description of the hardships faced by an individual afloat for ten days in an unprotected raft without provisions. Reminiscent of Hemingway's *Old Man and the Sea*, the narrative describes how the seaman is able to survive because of his good physical condition, his calmness in the face of adversity, and a determination probably born of military discipline (see his description on page 30 of how he reacts to being called a hero).

If the seaman's own ingenuous disclaimers give his statements merely the passing importance of a human-interest story, the basis on which *El Espectador* agreed to buy the story in the first place, how does *Relato* achieve importance as documentary narrative? García Márquez observes in his introduction that *El Espectador* and its eager reporter were unaware, when they reluctantly agreed to buy Velasco's story (they felt the topic had already been exhausted by the press), that it would unintentionally reveal an official cover-up of the events surrounding the incident. Whereas Velasco and seven other crewmen who drowned had been swept overboard in rough seas from the deck of a badly listing vessel, the official explanation was that they had been lost during an unexpected storm that made any rescue attempt impossible.

What had made the destroyer list dangerously in the rough seas of the open Caribbean between Cuba and Colombia was a heavy contraband cargo poorly distributed and inadequately lashed down on the deck. The cargo had been purchased in Mobile, Alabama, where the *Caldas* had been docked for eight months of repairs and refittings. The crewmen had used their pay from these long months in a foreign port for the purchase of household appliances and other goods; because of the double violation of transporting such cargo and transporting it on deck, the ship's officers were unquestionably compromised. Swept overboard when high waves broke the cargo loose, the seamen were left behind by a ship unable to maneuver in the rough seas because of its poorly distributed weight. When rescue planes found no trace of survivors, a storm was declared responsible, and the case was closed. Velasco's appearance ten days later did not alter this story, and the hero's welcome he received was perhaps unspoken compensation for his abandonment by the *Caldas*.

Nevertheless, in the subsequent re-creation of his story to

García Márquez, it soon became apparent that Velasco spoke of two details that did not jibe with the official versions: the *Caldas* carried heavy cargo on deck, and there had been no storm. The ensuing uproar—Colombia was ruled at the time by the dictator Gustavo Rojas Pinilla—cost Velasco his status as a hero and his job with the navy, sent García Márquez into the exile from which, ten years later, *Cien años de soledad* was to emerge, and resulted in *El Espectador* being closed down by the government. Thus, the documentary meaning of *Relato* derives not from Velasco's narrative as such but from both the accidental contradiction it provided of an official version of events and from García Márquez's subsequent recontextualization of the narrative in book form.

In the same way that the individual declarations gathered by Poniatowska provide little more than fragmentary versions of the events surrounding Tlatelolco and acquire their power as social and narrative document by virtue of the author's unifying conception, *Relato* derives its meaning from the manner in which García Márquez introduces it. Although García Márquez as narrator does not intervene in Velasco's story, we may assume that the subject's "natural" narrative is not altogether untainted by authorial intervention. The presence of the reporter-interviewer, the questions he may ask overtly, and the conditioning he may provide covertly and even unconsciously contribute to the configuration of the narrative.

García Márquez stresses the serendipitous nature of Velasco's revelations and how his story assumed the dimensions of an exposé:

> Lo que no sabíamos ni el náufrago ni yo cuando tratábamos de reconstruir minuto a minuto su aventura, era que aquel rastreo agotador había de conducirnos a una nueva aventura que causó un cierto revuelo en el país, que a él le costó su gloria y su carrera y que a mí pudo costarme el pellejo. . . .
>
> La historia, dividida en episodios, se publicó en catorce días consecutivos. El propio gobierno celebró al principio la consagración literaria de su héroe. Luego, cuando se publicó la verdad, habría sido una trastada política impedir que se continuara la serie: la circulación del periódico estaba casi doblada, y había frente al edificio una rebatiña de lectores que compraban los números atrasados para conservar la colección completa. La dictadura, de acuerdo con una tradición muy propia de los gobiernos colombianos, se conformó con remendar la verdad con la retórica: desmintió en un comunicado solemne que el destructor llevara mercancía de contra-

bando. . . . . La dictadura acusó el golpe con una serie de represalias drásticas que habían de culminar, meses después, con la clausura del periódico. (pp. 7, 9)

(What neither I nor the shipwreck knew when we attempted to reconstruct minute by minute his adventure was that that painstaking tracking would lead us to a new adventure that produced a certain uproar in the country, one that cost him his glory and could have cost me my skin. . . . The story, divided into episodes, was published on fourteen consecutive days. The government itself celebrated at first the literary consecration of its hero. Later, when the truth came out, it would have been political folly to ban the series: the circulation of the newspaper had doubled, and there were hoards of people in front of the building who bought up back numbers in order to save the whole collection. The dictatorship, in conformance with a very distinctive tradition among Colombian governments, contented itself with mending truth with rhetoric: in a solemn communiqué it denied that the destroyer had been carrying contraband merchandise. . . . The dictatorship responded to the blow with a series of drastic reprisals that would culminate, months later, with the closing of the newspaper.)

The text of *Relato* consists of Velasco's detailed reconstruction of the events leading up to his being swept overboard, his struggle to survive adrift at sea in a flimsy raft, and his subsequent rescue and canonization as a national hero. Read in conjunction with García Márquez's introduction, Velasco's representations assume dramatic irony because the reader has been informed what will happen and why: the reader's information is superior to that of Velasco not only at the time of the events he describes but also, significantly, at the time of his declarations to *El Espectador*'s reporter. For example, Velasco refers repeatedly to the crew's acquisition of articles to take back home, to their special relationship with a salesman in Mobile who, because he spoke excellent Spanish without ever having been in Latin America, was particularly favored with their money, and to the way the contraband initially protected the seaman on deck from the waves and then swept them overboard as it broke loose from its inadequate moorings. These references, read in conjunction with García Márquez's introduction, insistently foreshadow the impending disaster:

No quiero decir que desde ese instante [de ver la película *El motín del Caine*] empecé a presentir la catástrofe. Pero la verdad es que nunca había sentido tanto temor frente a la proximidad de un viaje.

En Bogotá, cuando era niño y veía las ilustraciones de los libros, nunca se me ocurrió que alguien pudiera encontrar la muerte en el mar. Por el contrario, pensaba en él con mucha confianza. Y desde cuando ingresé en la marina, hace casi doce años, no había sentido nunca ningún trastorno durante el viaje. . . . La inquietud me duró toda la semana. El día del viaje se aproximaba con alarmante rapidez y yo trataba de infundirme seguridad en la conversación con mis compañeros. El A.R.C. "Caldas" estaba listo para partir. Durante esos días se hablaba con más insistencia de nuestras familias, de Colombia y de nuestro[s] proyectos para el regreso. Poco a poco se iba cargando el buque con regalos que traíamos a nuestras casas: radios, neveras, lavadoras y estufas, especialmente. Yo traía un radio. (p. 12)

(I don't mean to say that from that instant [of seeing the movie *The Caine Mutiny*] I had the presentiment of the catastrophe. But the truth is that I had never been so frightened at an impending trip. In Bogotá, when I was a child and would see illustrations in books, it never occurred to me that someone could die at sea. On the contrary, I thought about the sea with confidence. And ever since joining the Navy, almost twelve years ago, I had never felt upset at sea. . . .

The uneasiness lasted all week for me. The day of the trip drew near with alarming rapidity, and I tried to shore my confidence up in conversation with my shipmates. The SS *Caldas* was ready to depart. During those days we all spoke with growing intensity of our families, of Colombia, and of our plans for our return. Little by little the ship filled up with gifts for home: radios, refrigerators, washing machines, and stoves, in particular. I was taking a radio back.)

What makes such unconscious foregrounding especially interesting is that Velasco maintains that he developed for the first time a fear of the sea (he and his shipmates had discussed, after seeing the *Caine Mutiny*, what they would do in such a storm). And he experiences a clear presentiment of the trouble on the voyage back to Colombia, a voyage both routine and short. Yet the references that foretell subsequent disaster at sea are based on the storm that serves as the narrative catalyst of the *Caine Mutiny* and not on the improper stowage of the contraband the crewmen purchased while they enjoyed movies and other relaxations ashore. The preoccupation with the storm at sea adds a further resonance: the government will cover the true circumstances of the seamen's fate by falsely attributing their loss to an unexpected storm.

On another level, the references to contraband become the

central point in the interplay between untrustworthy official versions and the truth of Velasco's narrative as unintentional exposé. Again, this relationship may only be perceived through the conjunction of the seaman's text and García Márquez's introduction. Two forms of contraband are symbolically interrelated in the text. There is the cargo stowed on deck in clear violation of military regulations. This cargo is the nucleus of Velasco's ordeal: its acquisition and quantity bespeak the long stay in Mobile away from home, and it is the reason the Caldas is unable to rescue the men swept overboard. This contraband, which the seaman mentions simply as the material cause of his ordeal with no thought to its illegality, triggers the "contraband" newspaper interviews: because they inadvertently reveal both the truth of the forbidden cargo and the lie concerning the storm at sea, El Espectador's articles become the object of persecution by the dictatorship. Truth is a contraband commodity in a repressive society, and reprisals for the "contraband" of Relato substitute for any judicial review against the officers of the Caldas and their accommodating superiors in the government. By the same token, the publication in 1970 of Relato acknowledges that its fundamental importance as a narrative document, beyond any intrinsic storytelling skills of the accidental literatus Luis Alejandro Velasco, derives from its unforeseen stature as contraband truth. It is this quality that makes Relato an appropriate example of Latin American documentary narrative.

VI

Miguel Barnet's Biografía de un cimarrón, published in 1966, exemplifies a subgenre of Caribbean literature that has acquired special prominence since the Castro revolution in Cuba in 1959: literature dealing with the black experience.[29] Slaves were introduced early in the Caribbean, when the indigenous population was unable to survive the harsh conditions imposed by the Spanish conquerors. Barnet (1942–), whose Canción de Rachel is one of the major narratives of the revolution, interviewed Esteban Montejo, a 105-year-old former slave who, after the abolition of slavery, became a peon on the sugarcane

29. See Ivan A. Schulman, "Reflections on Cuba and Its Antislavery Literature."

plantations that traditionally constituted the basis of Cuban economic wealth.[30] According to his own story, in an act of spontaneous rebellion he hurled a stone at one of the slave drivers and fled into the mountains, where he lived in solitude for several years as a runaway. Hence the epithet *cimarrón*, which is used in the Caribbean to denominate a runaway slave (similar to the English "maroon").

When he discovers that slavery has been abolished by the Spanish crown, Montejo returns to civilization and becomes a wage-earning peon. Barnet's presentation is misleadingly titled, because only a small portion of Montejo's narrative concerns his personal suffering as a slave and his subsequent experiences as a runaway. There are ample assertions concerning the dreadful subhuman lot of the slaves and the fact that conditions hardly improved after the formal abolition of slavery. But Montejo's story concentrates more on his interest in women, his descriptions of black folkways and customs in Cuba, traditional religious practices, and his own comings and goings, particularly his involvement in the struggle for Cuban independence from Spain that culminated in the American invasion of the island in 1898.[31]

Montejo's narrative, framed by Barnet's brief presentation, is perhaps the least novelistic of the documentary narratives I examine here.[32] Although it has been recognized as an important postrevolutionary text that is continuous with Barnet's creative

30. The difference between *Biografía* as a documentary narrative and *Canción* as a testimonial novel is instructive. The latter, told through the recollections of a fictional courtesan who is in retirement at the time of the 1959 Castro revolution, serves as the point of reference for the outlines of modern Cuban sociocultural history. See Raquel Chang-Rodríguez, "Sobre *La canción de Rachel*, novela-testimonio"; Miguel Barnet, "Miguel Barnet charla con los editores de *Vórtice*"; and Emilio Bejel, "Entrevista: Miguel Barnet." Angel Luis Fernández Guerra, "*Cimarrón* y *Rachel*, un 'continuum,'" is specifically concerned with the relationship between Barnet's two major works.

For a thorough analysis of *Biografía* as an example of the innovative contributions of Cuban narrative, see Roberto González Echevarría, "*Biografía de un cimarrón* and the Novel of the Cuban Revolution." Although González Echevarría focuses on *Biografía* as an example of the documentary novel, he emphasizes the sociocultural issue of "literature" versus history rather than the narrative strategies I stress here.

31. The continuing interest in Cuban slave literature is demonstrated by the recent publication of Juan Francisco Manzano's *The Life and Poems of a Cuban Slave*, ed. Edward J. Mullen (Hamden, Conn.: Archon Books, 1981).

32. The brief note by Manuel Moreno Fraginals, "*Biografía de un cimarrón*," focuses specifically on the ethnographic nature of *Biografía*, whose original publication in 1966 was by Havana's Instituto de Etnología y Folklore.

fiction, it clearly belongs to the tradition of personal memoirs of social life in Cuba, and Barnet introduces it as part of an ethnographic undertaking. By the same token, there can be little question that *Biografía* has an ulterior social motive: the documentation of both the authentic folk culture of Cuba that the revolution sought to recover and the deplorable human conditions that justify the revolution and its subsequent programs.

Montejo's symbolic status as a rebel against the institution of slavery, his participation in the struggle for Cuban independence, his membership in the Cuban Socialist party, and, above all else, his representations of the solidarity of the black slave society and subsequently the black ethnic minority all attest to values promoted by the official mythopoesis of the Castro government. Thus, the correspondences between Montejo's declarations and the overall coherence of his narrative acquire meaning within the context of postrevolutionary Cuban society by evoking intertextually an entire range of social and artistic documents.

If the postrevolutionary culture in Cuba constitutes a body of intertexts for the appropriate reading of Montejo's story, the ethnographic framework is a subtext that reveals the interplay between autobiographical documentary and social narrative. In a tone that would strike an American post-civil-rights-movement reader as somewhat patronizing, Barnet describes his early meetings with Montejo. The old man rambled on repetitively and without regard for chronology. After he had established the essential interest of the former's slave story, Barnet claims that he prepared an inventory of chronologically based questions concerning the principal topics covered by Montejo's earlier statements. The man's replies to these questions were recorded, polished, and published as *Biografía*. The editorial process involved a minimum of correction in order to retain the man's style and his sociolect, which includes archaisms, regionalisms, and socioeducationally determined solecisms. Barnet provides an appendix of vocabulary the nonspecialist reader might not recognize and footnotes clarifying some of the historical references.

There are several major problems with this framework. In the first place, the narrative cannot be read as a spontaneous declaration, free of intervening interpretation. Aside from the conditions imposed by the presence of the ethnographic interviewer and the instruments of his stenographic or electronic transcription, Barnet makes it clear that what is presented as Montejo's autobiography is a second version elicited by questions based on the first, more rambling statements. However, Barnet's questions are not presented in *Biografía* as either an integral part of the text or as an appendix. Montejo's narrative is divided into three segments of unequal length—"La esclavitud" (Slavery), "La abolición de la esclavitud" (Abolition of Slavery), and "La guerra de la independencia" (War of Independence)—along with untitled internal divisions of diverse length. There is no way in which the reader can reconstruct Barnet's questions, except by the rather unproductive process of generating questions based on discrete statements: When Montejo states, "A mí nunca se me ha olvidado la primera vez que intenté huirme" (I can never forget the first time I attempted to escape; p. 42), the reader can assume a hypothetical question posed by Barnet: "Tell me about the first time you attempted to escape." Reminiscent of that novelistic technique whereby one speaker's words are transcribed while another's are represented by ellipses, *Biografía* presents as explicit text a narrative generated by a subtext conditioned by an interviewer's questions based on avowed ethnographic motives and confessed sociopolitical interests:

> Como nuestro interés primordial radicaba en aspectos generales de las religiones de origen africano que se conservan en Cuba, tratamos al principio de indagar sobre ciertas particularidades. No fue difícil lograr un diálogo vivo, utilizando, desde luego, los recursos habituales de la investigación etnológica.[33]

> Su tradición de revolucionario, cimarrón primero, luego libertador, miembro del Partido Socialista Popular más tarde, se vivifica en nuestros días en su identificación con la Revolución cubana.
> Este libro no hace más que narrar vivencias comunes a muchos hombres de su misma nacionalidad. La etnología las recoge para los estudiosos del medio social, historiadores y folkloristas.
> Nuestra satisfacción mayor es la de reflejarlas a través de un legítimo actor del proceso histórico cubano. (p. 12)

> (Since our basic interest lies with general features of the religions of African origin preserved in Cuba, we attempted at first to delve into certain peculiarities. It was not difficult to establish a lively dialogue making use, of course, of all of the usual techniques of ethnological investigation.

33. Miguel Barnet, *Biografía de un cimarrón*, 2d ed., p. 7. Further citations will be given in the text.

His experiences as a revolutionary, first as a runaway slave, then as a freedom fighter, a member of the People's Socialist party, later came alive in the present because of his identification with the Cuban Revolution. This book does no more than relate life experiences common to many men and his own nationality. Ethnology collects those experiences for researchers of the social setting, historians, and folklorists. Our greatest satisfaction is that of reflecting them in the person of a legitimate participant in the Cuban historical process.)

These avowals of legitimate anthropological concern are accompanied by the disclaimer that Barnet's intent is to write literature. This disclaimer is strategically important because of Barnet's identification with the contemporary Cuban novel. However, it follows his frank admission that, in presenting Montejo's autobiography, he has added an intervening level between Montejo's spontaneous declarations and the text we receive. In addition to restructuring the "natural narrative" through ethnographic questions, Barnet has felt constrained to copyedit the transcript for greater concisensss (compare p. 10). These decisions, made by a highly skilled novelist, undoubtedly enhance Montejo's narrative. And in the process, although they do not justify our reading *Biografía* as pseudoanthropological fiction, they lend it a novelistic texture that disrupts significantly its "raw" documentary value.

The dominant narrative marker in *Biografía* is the controlling predicate statement "Yo vide" (I saw). It is immaterial whether this recurring phrase is consciously or unconsciously uttered, whether it is Montejo's own or Barnet's attribution. That it is one of the principal archaisms in the text lends it an added emphasis (it is archaic Spanish for "yo vi"), and it clearly punctuates the narrative as an attribution of authenticity. By the same token, it is carefully counterbalanced by statements to the effect that such-and-such an event or circumstance was not actually witnessed by the narrator ("Eso no lo vide yo, pero me lo contaron"). That is, there is a very clear interplay between what the narrator can claim as true by virtue of personal experience and what he can only report as claimed by others. In turn, such a "reportorial humility" further authenticates his story because it lends credence to what Montejo claims are personal experiences. This is especially true when he refers to what the modern reader would likely take as traditional superstitions rather than verifiable facts:

Pero el sol es más importante, porque él es el que le da vida a la luna. Con el sol trabajaban los congos casi todos los días. Cuando tenían algún problema con alguna persona, ellos seguían a esa persona por el trillo cualquiera y recogían el polvo que ella pisaba. Lo guardaban y lo ponían en la nganga o en un rinconcito. Según el sol iba bajando, la vida de la persona se iba yendo. Y a la puesta del sol la persona estaba muertecita. Yo digo esto porque da por resultado que yo lo vide mucho en la esclavitud. (p. 32)

(But the sun is more important because it is he who gives life to the moon. The Congolese worked magic with the sun almost every day. When they had trouble with a particular person they would follow him along a path, collect up some of the dust he walked upon and put it in the *nganga* or in some little secret place. As the sun went down that person's life would begin to ebb away, and at sunset he would be dying. I mention this because it is something I often saw under slavery.)[34]

Throughout his autobiography, Montejo recognizes the importance of his memory, for it gives continuity to his story and coherence to the information he is relaying, to the extent that he can relate his personal experiences to a specific sociohistorical panorama of Cuba:

Aunque estuve unos cuantos años en Ariosa, las cosas se han olvidado un poco. Lo mejor que hay para la memoria es el tiempo. El tiempo conserva los recuerdos. Cuando uno quiere acordarse de las cosas del tiempo nuevo, no puede. Sin embargo, mientras más atrás uno mire, más claro lo ve todo. (p. 88)

(Although I stayed several years at Ariosa I am beginning to forget things about it now. Time is the best help for the memory. If you try to remember something which happened recently you can't, but the further back you go the more clearly you see it all.) (p. 96)

As a consequence, the narrator is able to stipulate repeatedly the disjunction between the historical reality he clearly recalls and the imperfect memory of people today or between that historical reality and the changes that have occurred in Cuban society:

Me los amarraron fuertes [los grillos] y me pusieron a trabajar con ellos y todo. Uno dice eso ahora y la gente no lo cree. Pero yo lo sentí y lo tengo que decir. (p. 16)

34. *The Autobiography of a Runaway Slave: Esteban Montejo*, trans. Jacosta Innes, p. 34. Further translations from *Biografía* are from this edition and will be cited in the text.

Antes las flores gustaban mucho. Dondequiera había flores. Hoy no se ven como en aquellos días de las fiestas. Yo me acuerdo que todas las casas estaban adornadas con flores. (p. 71)

Yo veo eso como una prueba de amistad. Hoy la gente no se comporta así. Hay la envidia y los celos por dondequiera. (p. 143)

[But they caught me without a struggle, clapped a pair of shackles on me (I can still feel them when I think back), screwed them up tight and sent me back to work wearing them. You talk about this sort of thing today and people don't believe you, but it happened to me and I have to say so.] (p. 18)

(Flowers were very popular then, there were flowers everywhere. You never see flowers now like there were on fiesta days. They were used to decorate all the houses.) (p. 77)

(I see all this as proof of friendship. People don't behave like that nowadays. Everywhere you look now there is envy and jealousy.) (p. 158)

Montejo's overriding concern—as it is of any individual, fictional or otherwise, who tells his "own story"—is to explain how things were. His goal is to interpret for his audience (Barnet, in immediate terms; the anonymous reader of the text, in general) the nature of his life and what he understands it to represent within the context of the blacks' experience in Cuba as slaves and second-class citizens. Although the resulting texture is narrative primarily because it has as an organizing point of reference the specific life of the first-person narrator, with little dramatic or action narrative, *Biografía* is a documentary with the undeniable novelistic traces I have outlined.

VII

It should be apparent that a clear unity underlies the five works I have examined as representative of documentary narrative: all depend, for their one defining structural principle, on the productive interfacing of a narrative explicitly framed by an author but attributable to historically "real" individuals. There exists a sociopolitical continuity in the Latin American novel from its earliest origins in the late-Renaissance chronicles of the Conquest, and there exists an overwhelming testimonial quality about the dominant strands of contemporary Latin American literature. Hence, any definition of documentary literature must go beyond the referential links between historical events and texts.

Rather than pursuing a nebulous classification based on degrees of fictionality and referentiality, I have sought to identify those texts in which a credibly "real" story is given an explicit narrative framework by an intervening narrator. Not insignificantly, these narrators are acknowledged and often well-known novelists. Thus, although I have avoided the question of fictionality by concentrating on essentially nonfictional documents, I have given special prominence to the issue of narrativity, the ways acknowledged novelists frame their narratives and use standard narrative strategies such as complementary and contrapuntal juxtaposition (Poniatowska and Walsh), irony (García Márquez and Valdés), authorial "editing" and commentary (Walsh and Barnet), and disjunctive interplay between levels of text like natural discourse and transcribed narrative (Barnet and Valdés). These strategies do not make these five texts novels any more than the parables and other varieties of narrative make the Bible a novel. Rather, by invoking and echoing the structuring principles of mainstream contemporary Latin American novels, they underscore the continuity between imaginative literature and documentary in Latin American culture.

VIII

Appendix: A Brazilian Semidocumentary

It is disappointing that there is no clear example of documentary narrative in Brazil. However, we should not expect to find the same forms of narrative in Brazil that we find in Spanish-speaking Latin America, or vice-versa. Just as Brazil manifests some outstanding examples of science-fiction, without there being any clearly comparable works in Mexico or Argentina, Brazilian writers seem not to have followed Spanish-American novelists in employing documentary narrative to portray a complex sociopolitical reality.

To be sure, events in Brazil have been no less noteworthy than those on the rest of the continent, and the historian or journalist would not be hard put to suggest stories that might lend themselves to documentary treatment. Where documentary narrative did emerge in Brazil as a major force was not in the novel but in the theater, with Augusto Boal's Teatro Jornal.[35] When Boal, who is both a dramatist and an original dramatic theoretician, left Brazil because of government harassment, he carried his ideas for a documentary theater to other parts of Latin America.

There is, however, one example of Brazilian semidocumentary narrative that deserves attention. José Louzeiro's *Aracelli meu amor: um anjo espera a justiça dos homens* (1976). Although I have not been able to locate any critical commentaries on this work,[36] it has attracted enough attention to warrant four printings in five years, and a 1980 stage version enjoyed considerable success. Interestingly, the theatrical interpretation of *Aracelli* was more documentary than the novel, perhaps because of the abiding influence of Boal among serious theatrical producers.

Aracelli is a crime story, and, like the other examples of documentary narrative I examined above, American libraries classify it as nonfiction. Louzeiro re-creates the case of a little girl, Aracelli Cabrera Campos, who disappeared on her way home from school in Vitória (north of Rio de Janeiro) on the afternoon of 18 May 1973. Although her body was found in a ravine and credible accusations were formulated, no one ever stood trial for the crime, and the file continues open to this day. Following three people—two dedicated policemen (one of whom was himself murdered under suspicious circumstances) and an old and eccentric gypsy woman—who individually pursue the clues and interpret them, the narrative re-creates the circumstances of the child's death and the various official and extra-official attempts to identity the guilty and bring them to justice.

The narrative leaves little doubt as to the actual events: Aracelli's mother cooperated with a group of sons of rich and influential businessmen in allowing her daughter to be corrupted by sex and drugs to liven the young men's parties. During one of these orgies, Aracelli apparently lost consciousness from an overdose of drugs, and attempts to revive her failed. The men

35. Augusto Boal, "Teatro jornal: primeira edição," *Latin American Theatre Review* 4, no. 2 (1971):57–60.
36. The only reference on Louzeiro I have been able to find is the review of his novel *Lúcio Flávio: o passageiro da agonia* by Ramão Gomes Portão. *Lúcio Flávio* was made into a movie by the Argentine director Héctor Babenco. The text, which deals with a bankrobber persecuted by the death squads, is marked by an annoying mawkishness that must be intended to redeem what is otherwise a not very heroic social type.

disfigured her body and dumped it in the ravine hoping it would not be found or identified. When it was, their fathers' influence assured that they would never come to trial, despite the dogged work of a few detectives and a public inquiry held by a congressman of the opposition party when the corrupt government appeared unwilling to act.

Louzeiro's narrative is problematical as a documentary, despite its obvious identification with the genre. Although a few newspaper articles are included, they are not set off as such but are read aloud by the characters or quoted indirectly in conversations and arguments. The testimony of the witnesses at the public inquiry is quoted independently; presumably the citations are verbatim, but there is no evidence to this effect. Since the novel is structured in terms of the overlapping investigations of the two detectives and the gypsy woman, Louzeiro frequently makes use of interior monologue and free direct quotation. This material could have been obtained through interviews with the parties concerned, and it would then constitute documentary material by presenting what they claimed to have thought, said, and overheard (as in the case of Walsh's narrative or Poniatowksa's clearly identified interviews). Whether this is the case or whether Louzeiro has engaged in the extensive fictional re-creation typical of historical novels is not discernible.

Aside from naming in the dedication the two police officers who took a sincere professional interest in the case, Louzeiro includes no documentary corroboration or justification, which implies that he did not feel constrained to frame his narrative explicitly as documentary. This is hardly to the detriment of his text; it only means that the reader is more likely to approach it as a verisimilar fictional metaphor than as an interpretation of sociopolitical fact. Since one of the goals of documentary narrative, quite apart from proving the old adage that truth is stranger than fiction, is to disprove the allegation that writers deal only with artful and fanciful lies, the immediacy of the form is considerably attenuated, if not lost, in Louzeiro's work.

Louzeiro's decision not to use explicit documentary framing, beyond the concrete references to the circumstances of the case that serve to recall to many readers the reports read in the press at the time, allows for the foregrounding of traditional novelistic devices: a narrative mosaic that shifts from one setting to another, from one character to another, from reported speech to interior monologue; the extensive use by the narrator of pathetic fallacy in eliciting pity and outrage over Aracelli's horrible fate; and, most disruptive in terms of a documentary texture, the interruption of the factual narrative by the otherworldly events surrounding the gypsy woman. The conflict here is not that between a Brazilian and a foreign attitude toward gypsy arts. Rather, the issue is the disjunction of documentary fact and secret miracle. Moreover, one of the two principal investigators is bothered precisely by this disjunction. Because the gypsy, Rita, believes both that God rather than man will punish the guilty and that the girl's murder is a sign of the corruption of the times, the segments that diverge from the framework of journalistic reconstruction of objective fact assume the eloquence of a novelistic metaphor concerning the decay of modern Brazilian society:

—Cada vez mais a situação se complica. Não vejo como se desvendar esse caso—queixa-se Dudu, num dos raros momentos de desânimo.

—Também já não vejo saída—diz Rita Soares.—Por isso é que acho que o caso tá entregue a Deus. Só dele vem o castigo. Mas, como muita gente já não acredita em Deus, todo mundo por aqui continua se mexendo pra encontrar uma solução. . . . Era até engraçado se Deus tivesse se preocupando de dar satisfação pra gente.[37]

("This business gets more and more complicated all the time. I don't see how to unravel this case," Dudu complained, during one of his rare moments of disheartenment.

"I can't see any way out, either," Rita Soares says. "That's why I think the matter is in God's hands. Only from him will punishment come. But, since so many people don't believe in God anymore, everyone around here continues to run around looking for an answer. . . . It would even be funny if God bothered to give people any satisfaction.")

From a documentary point of view, Louzeiro does use two narrative strategies that ally his novel with the other texts we have considered: (1) the repetition of tropes of frustration at not being able to fit the pieces together and to establish an unambiguous interpretation of the elements of the case; and (2) the development of the basic deviations from an accepted social

37. José Louzeiro, *Aracelli, meu amor; um anjo espera a justiça dos homens*, 4th ed., p. 137 (Dudu is one of the police investigators). Further citations will be given in the text.

norm that the actual event reveals. Fiction is characterized by its ability to articulate or explain a complex event or situation, and it is in crime or detective fiction that we most often see the pieces fitting together and a "final" explanation offered—by Perry Mason in his office, Sherlock Holmes in his study, or Phillip Marlowe in a seedy bar—in a way that eloquently counterpoises the uncertainties of "real" life. *Aracelli* does not wrap events up, nor do we have the satisfaction of seeing justice rendered: if Aracelli is a paradigm for the victimization of the innocent individual in corrupt and degrading modern Brazil, the circumstances of social life that permitted her rape and the continued liberty of the guilty still "await the justice of men." Significantly, the author's subtitle ignores the gypsy Rita's faith in the wrath of God, and, thereby, provides an unequivocal sociopolitical context for the events narrated.

However, to the extent that Aracelli's case remains unclosed, in the same way that Brazil remains a corrupt and unjust society, the narrative is punctuated by variations on the theme of despair in the face of limited knowledge and our inability to make sense out of facts, near facts, contradictory facts, and assorted allegations:

—Confesso que não tou entendendo nada—afirma o detetive Matos—ou a própria mãe da criança tá procurando confundir as investigações. (p. 23)

—É difícil dizer. Tá tudo muito nebuloso. (p. 68)

—Pra mim, as implicações não podem ser tão simples quanto imaginamos. (p. 96)

Qualquer coisa naquele amontoado de palavras é, de fato, importante. Numa fração de segundo, no espaço de uma palavra para a outra, está a verdade. Mas que verdade? Como supreendê-la? Fecha os olhos, os ruídos dos carros descendo a ladeira chegam até o apartamento, o suave toque dos sinos assinala as horas. (p. 163)

("I confess that I don't get any of it," Detective Moros asserts, "unless the girl's mother herself is trying to confuse the investigation."

"It's difficult to say. Everything is very cloudy."

"As far as I am concerned, the implications can't be as simple as we think they are."

Anything in that jumble of words is, in fact, important. In a fraction of a second, in the space between two words, lies the truth. But what truth? How to surprise it? He closes his eyes, and the noises of the cars descending the slope rise to the apartment, the soft sound of the chimes marks the hour.)

It is important that the search for the truth becomes an antagonistic struggle between the agents of the powerful, who wish to bury the matter or to find a scapegoat (at one point, they attempt to pin the blame on a hapless bum), and a handful of decent, if powerless, individuals who encounter nothing but obstacles in their way. One detective working on the case is killed under unexplained circumstances, evidence disappears, Aracelli's parents become uncooperative, witnesses are intimidated, and pressure from unspecified higher sources is brought to bear. In this way, like crime fiction in the Raymond Chandler and Dashiell Hammett tradition, *Aracelli* allows exploration of the social conflicts that underlie the case, the unprotected child exploited and corrupted by the sons of the powerful:

—Nós tamos de baixo. Tamos do lado em que os ricos cospem. Nossa desgraça é sua alegria. Mas por este crime os magnatas de Vitória vão se arrepender. E se, por acaso, a Justiça se abrandar contra eles, invoco aqui os nossos santos protetores pra que eles sofram os horrores do inferno nesta vida mesmo. Que seu sofrimento seja resposta ao nosso pedido. (p. 65; the words belong to the opposition congressman)

("We've hit bottom. We're downwind from where the rich spit. Our misfortune is their joy. But the magnates of Vitória are going to be sorry for this crime. And if, by chance, Justice against them weakens, I hereby invoke our patron saints to make them suffer the horrors of hell in this very life. Let their suffering be the answer to our request.")

The social denunciation and the portrait of a debased society are underscored by the deviations from an accepted social norm that the case reveals. If the norms—the societal myths that go unquestioned until an Aracelli is victimized—affirm the protection of the innocent, the comfort of the family, and the persecution of the guilty, *Aracelli* charts the significant deviations from such norms that are revealed by the case. The orgiastic corruption of a minor, the hedonistic pursuits of the children of the powerful, the complicity of a parent in the sexual exploitation of her own child, police indifference encouraged by the authorities—even if the realistic or the cynical accept these as sociopolitical facts of life, they are deviations from the public social norm that Louzeiro's narrative plays on. That the deviations are revealed by the complex facts of an actual event is, of course, the point of emphasis to be gained by treating an allegedly real happening. The denunciation of modern Brazilian society that emerges from Louzeiro's version of documentary fiction is found in the irony arising from the abyss between the avowal by authorities that the case will be solved and justice done and their complicity with the guilty, between the mother's cry of despair (—Minha filha! Que fizeram com ela! [p. 5]) and the truth about her involvement, and between the outpouring of public rage over the crime and the impenetrable curtain of silence drawn over it. Rather than an interpretation or clarification of a documentary event through the use of novelistic strategies, although the general truth is inescapable by the conclusion of the text, Louzeiro's *Aracelli* is primarily the chronicle of a frustrated quest for social justice through the resolution of one perfidious act that lays bare the corruption of an entire society.

2. Narrative Persona in Eva Perón's *La razón de mi vida*

No vaya a creerse por esto que digo que la tarea de Evita me resulte fácil. Más bien me resulta en cambio siempre difícil y nunca me he sentido del todo contenta con esa actuación. En cambio el papel de Eva Perón me parece fácil. Y no es extraño. ¿Acaso no resulta siempre más fácil representar un papel en el teatro que vivirlo en la realidad?[1]

(Do not think by this that "Evita's" work comes easily to me. Rather, it always turns out to be difficult, and I have never felt quite satisfied in that role. On the other hand, the part of Eva Perón seems easy. And it is not strange. For is it not always easier to act a stage part than to live it in person?) (p. 63)

I

The Peronista period may not have stimulated the production of many works of lasting literary merit,[2] but it did produce one document of undeniable paraliterary interest: Eva Duarte Perón's *La razón de mi vida* (1951). The paraliterary nature of this book lies neither in the questionable quality of its expressive style nor in the presumedly overt fictionality of the "facts" it purports to set forth and interpret. Rather, in this essay I will examine *Razón* as a paraliterary text for (1) the discourse struc-

---

1. Eva Perón, *La razón de mi vida*, p. 94. All quotes are from the edition given in the bibliography and will be cited by page number within the text. Translations are taken from Eva Duarte Perón, *Evita by Evita: Eva Duarte Perón Tells Her Own Story*. No translator is specified.
2. Concerning the literature of Peronismo, see Ernesto Goldar, "La literatura peronista," in *El peronismo*, pp. 139–86, and Martin S. Stabb, "Argentine Letters and the Peronato: An Overview." See also Goldar's *El peronismo en la literatura argentina* and Andrés Oscar Avellaneda, "El tema del peronismo en la narrativa argentina." An interesting "derivative" of *La razón de mi vida* is the long poem based on it by Leonidas Lamborghini, "Eva Perón en la hoguera," in his *Partitas* (Buenos Aires: Corregidor, 1972), pp. 53–71.

45

tures it manipulates to create a narrative persona that gives coherence to the story told and (2) its value as an implicit contribution to written popular culture in Argentina. This contribution arises both from the specific figure of Eva Perón that *Razón* propagates (its contribution of the myth of Eva Perón inside and outside Argentina)[3] and from what it implies about the criteria of the Argentine reading public for written literature.[4] (*Literature* is used here in the broad sense of written texts, without reference to the pretensions at fictionality—a relative rather than absolute distinction—and at identification with the norms of high culture.)[5]

It is necessary to distinguish between Eva Perón as author of *Razón* and Eva Perón as the narrative persona of that text; whether that persona is fictional or accurate in some usefully documentary fashion will have to depend on the assessment of professional historians.[6] It matters little, therefore, whether the "real" Eva Perón authored the text published under her name: Eva Perón the author is as much a product of political fiction as Eva Perón the narrator is a product of narrative fiction.

3. The many images of Eva Perón are examined in the anthropological study by J. M. Taylor, *Eva Perón: The Myths of a Woman.* Alberto Ciria also examines varying interpretations of Eva's personality in "Flesh and Fantasy: The Many Faces of Evita (and Juan Perón)." There has been a rash of recent book publications on Eva Perón. The majority of them border on yellow journalism and are not pertinent to this study. Several Argentine studies also available on Eva Perón are listed in Taylor's bibliography. One publication, titled *Eva Perón* and typical of the revisionist interpretations of Eva Perón by the Argentine left in the midseventies, is not listed by Taylor. One of the best Argentine studies is still Juan José Sebreli's interpretation of Evita as an authentic revolutionary, *Eva Perón ¿aventureraa o militante?* Sebreli discusses in passing the question of the real authorship of *Razón.* The first popular-culture analysis of Eva is provided by William Katra in "Eva Perón: Popular ♡ueen of Hearts," which quotes from *Razón* extensively. Katra has provided a more extensive characterization of the popular elements of Eva's figure in "Eva Perón: Media Queen of the Peronist Working Class." See also the comments by Ernesto Goldar on Eva Perón's *Historia del peronismo*: "Eva Perón: una filosofía de la historia," in his *La descolonización ideológica*, pp. 127–33. Finally, Lucia Fischer-Pap's *Eva: Theodora. Evita Peron: Empress Theodora Incarnated* reads (unintentionally, I am willing to assume) like drugstore-rack "real" stories.

4. There are only fragmentary studies on the Argentine reading public. One of the most authoritative is Adolfo Prieto, *Sociología del público argentino.* See my analysis of Prieto's work in "Adolfo Prieto: Profile of a Parricidal Literary Critic," *Latin American Research Review* 13 (1978):125–45.

5. For issues related to this position, see Barbara Herrnstein Smith, *On the Margins of Discourse: The Relation of Literature to Language.*

6. For a discussion of the interpenetration of "literary" and "historical" versions of "real" events and persons, see Hayden V. White, *Tropics of Discourse: Essays in Cultural History.*

Rather than with the documentary relationship among reality, author, and narrative persona, I will be concerned here with the narrative principles that underlie *Razón*. These strategies serve to elaborate and maintain the image of a coherent narrative persona. Attention will also be directed to the textual markers—rhetorical procedures, stylistic devices, structural features—that enhance that image by imposing on the reader a particular way of reading and understanding the text. Concomitantly, such an analysis will address the issue of how *Razón* is an example of Argentine popular culture, not so much from the point of view of the sociopolitical goals that publication of the text may have had, but from that of the reader codes it implies.[7]

II

The distinction between Eva Perón, author, and Eva Perón, narrator, is especially necessary in attempting to answer one of the fundamental questions raised concerning a text: How does it justify itself? How does it defend its claim to our attention?[8] Clearly, *La razón de mi vida* was published as part of the propaganda program of the Peronista government, and Evita's death within seven months of the book's publication made it particularly useful in the process of mythification and beatification of her person to which the government turned in the frantic attempt to shore up its crumbling power.

As a political tract, *Razón* was but one element in a continuing political struggle, used specifically as required reading in

7. I have been unable to find a useful study of *Razón* in the extensive literature on Peronismo. Mention should be made, however, of José R. Liberal's "scholarly" propaganda: *Eva Perón: estudio literario y valoración sociológica de "La razón de mi vida."* In short chapters that parallel *Razón*, Liberal offers a superficial explication of the book, without any literary or sociological analysis. It is, however, noteworthy that Liberal does conceive of approaching *Razón* from a literary point of view, no matter how ineffectual his comments in fact are. There has been a lot of attention in recent years to "reader codes" for both literary and nonliterary texts. One major statement is Roland Barthes, *S/Z*, and the issues are summarized by Jonathan Culler, *Structuralist Poetics: Structuralism, Linguistics, and the Study of Literature*. A somewhat different approach is provided by Wolfgang Iser, who is concerned with how the meaning of the text, rather than being inherent, is realized by the act of reading: *The Implied Reader; Patterns of Communication in Prose Fiction from Bunyan to Beckett*.
8. The principles of discourse contracts are discussed by Mary Louise Pratt in her *Toward a Speech Act Theory of Literary Discourse* and by Teun A. van Dijk in *Pragmatics of Language and Literature*.

Argentine public schools.[9] In this sense, the text does not need to expound or to imply intrinsic justifications: it circulated widely not because of the inherent eloquence of its rhetorical strategies but because it was imposed on one group of readers and insinuated itself with another by virtue of its participation in a range of myth-making activities surrounding the figure of Eva Perón. Beyond the reasonable assumption that millions of students read it because it was an obligatory textbook, there is no reliable index of how many purchasers actually read it and derived either an aesthetic or intellectual satisfaction from doing so.

By contrast, read today without either the political or the emotional coercion that supported its publication thirty years ago, *Razón*, as a discourse text that must justify any claim to our attention, may be approached in terms of the pretensions at privileged communication by Eva Perón the narrator. All discourse texts are forms of privileged communication in the sense that they lay claims to our attention; if we read or listen to them, we are according them the "privilege" of our interest. In return, the text must justify that privilege by complying with criteria of interest, conciseness, adequate exposition, and the like. Texts rarely address themselves overtly to how they are justified, although the storyteller's trope, "Listen to the marvelous tale I am about to tell, for you have never heard anything like it before," is one example of a direct identification of the text's inherent appeal to the audience's interest. More customarily, texts employ oblique or subtle references to the unique validity of their interest to us. And many of these presentational strategies are, in addition to elements of stylistic enhancement, procedures for implying how the text views its interest and its uniqueness.

One of the salient features of *Razón* supports the foregoing observations concerning narrative privilege and self-justification. Unlike historical, autobiographical, or documentary texts, *Razón* does not claim to be an interpretation of the real-life events it refers to. The literature on any major political event is

---

9. Goldar, in his section on "Evita," mentions a story by David Viñas, "El privilegiado," in which, among other indignities, a schoolteacher is required to read and teach *Razón* (p. 65). I have record of two school textbooks on *Razón* that indicate the sort of materials prepared for the teaching of Evita's narrative: Graciela Albornoz de Videla, *Evita: libro de lectura para 1 grado inferior*, and Adelina Cantarella, *Guía para análisis analógico de "La razón de mi vida" de Eva Perón*.

filled with analyses by impartial observers, by interested parties, by prominent participants. Peronismo is no exception.

However, against the wealth of material propounding this and that interpretation of the movement, *Razón* is characterized not only by its reference to specific events but also by its lack of interest in analyzing them or discussing the narrator's own intervention in them. That is to say, unlike a conventional autobiography, *Razón* does not pretend to chronicle the successive events of Eva Perón's life and the details of her participation in the major activities of her husband's government. True, there are references to recognizable occurrences and comments concerning Eva's involvement with them, like her attempts to free Perón after his arrest in October 1945 (chapters 8 and 9). The reader of a conventional biography would eagerly expect to have Eva's version of what happened, what she did, what was said, along with an explanation of the complex emotions she must have felt. Yet, aside from references to the bare facts of what occurred, the reader receives only a general statement regarding the woman's intense efforts on Perón's behalf and her overall sense of elation in the face of her relationship with the Leader.

Indeed, the historical and personal events described by *Razón* can only be followed adequately by a reader already familiar with the "history" underlying the text, either through direct knowledge of occurrences, as was the original audience of the book, or through documentary information provided by the large body of writings about the Peróns, as is the current reader. But, if interpretational (auto)biography or historical documentary is not the goal of *Razón*, what is? How does the narrator justify the privilege of her discourse?

The first of the fifty-nine chapters closes with the following words:

> Yo misma quiero explicarme aquí.
> Para eso he decidido escribir estos apuntes.
> Confieso que no lo hago para contradecir o refutar a nadie.
> ¡Quiero más bien que los hombres y las mujeres de mi pueblo sepan cómo siento y cómo pienso. . .!
> Quiero que sientan conmigo las cosas grandes que mi corazón experimenta.
> Seguramente, muchas de las cosas que diré son enseñanzas que yo recibí gratuitamente de Perón y que no tengo tampoco derecho a guardar como un secreto. (p. 14)

(I would like to make myself clear about this.
That is why I have decided to write these notes.
But I do not do so to contradict anyone or to prove anyone wrong.
Rather I would wish my fellow citizens, men and women, to know how I feel and think.
I want them to share in the great things I experience in my heart.
Surely many of the things I shall say here are teachings I received freely from Perón and which I have not the right to keep secret.)
(pp. 3–4)

Thus, Eva does not set out to refute or contradict the many scurrilous opinions that had circulated concerning her origins and her objectives (although there are, in fact, several direct and indirect allusions to views she feels compelled specifically to repudiate). Rather, she provides an accurate portrait of the feelings, emotions, and sentiments that distinguish her from her mentor (Juan Perón), from her enemies, and, indeed, from the entire Peronista movement. The basis of such a distinction is the "reason" of her intuitive feelings, which are presented as virtually paradigmatic of conventional feminine emotiveness. Read in terms of present-day feminist movements, Eva's self-portrait is as unconsciously parodic as it is paradigmatic of the shibboleths concerning masculine mind versus feminine heart.

Razón is not organized in accord with any discernible logic of metahistorical or philosophical discourse, and we have already discussed how it does not follow the outlines of an autobiographical narrative. Presented in vignettes that run four to five pages apiece, the work emphasizes key topics of Eva's participation in the Peronista movement. As a consequence, the image that emerges of the narrator's appeal to the reader is essentially fragmentary, without either the reasoned exposition one associates with a political essay or the concentrated, systematic symbolism characteristic of self-conscious literature. Nevertheless, a general pattern underlies *Razón* and supports the narrator's claim to our attention by reinforcing a coherent persona for her. This persona sees herself as essentially unique, possessing a sense of mission and a depth of perception vis-à-vis that mission that sets Eva Perón, the historical figure, apart from the rest of her countrymen, and, therefore, makes her story a privileged version of events. This persona seeks to demonstrate how she embodies a range of "natural"—and presumably more authentic—feelings that refute the worn and corrupt prejudices of traditional culture in Argentina. And this persona promotes a level of intuitive knowledge that makes her narrative valuable as an interpretation that only she can provide. The most important of these distinctions concerns that of the "natural" versus the "cultural," a distinction that reinforces not only the uniqueness of Eva's role, in contrast to the masculine— and military—logic of Perón's leadership, but also the primacy of her sincerity, in contrast to the "mediocrity" of her enemies. In such a formulation, the patterns of culture—the myths and rituals by which a society defines what is proper versus what is unacceptable and confers meaning on the former while denying it to the latter—are seen as arbitrary conventions that stifle the "natural" spontaneity of man. All societies develop codes of cultural behavior (and, in the course of history, borrow from each other). The classic mind defends them as necessary for imposing order on chaotic human drives, while the romantic mind denounces their tyranny because they shackle the natural, creative impulses of mankind.[10]

Razón uses this dichotomy to range the oppressiveness of traditional Argentine culture, with its roots in the French and English elite and its rigorous class distinctions, against the freedom inherent in Justicialismo, Peronismo's official but vaguely defined political doctrine. The latter seeks to destroy degrading social categories and to dignify man, who, in the purity of the pursuit of decency without pretensions, is viewed as fundamentally good. The discrimination against the poor by the oligarchy, which dismisses the former as "animal-like" and lacking in the higher sentiments of civilized man, are refuted in favor of the image of the *descamisado* as a noble innocent whose sentiments are all the more profound because of their ingenuousness:

> Yo he oído muchas veces en boca de "gente bien", como ellos suelen llamarse a sí mismos, cosas como éstas:
> —No se aflija tanto por sus "descamisados". Esa "clase de gente"

---

10. The study of "nature" versus "culture" and the structuring of myths of the latter that account for the former have been major contributions of Claude Lévi-Strauss's anthropological theories. One of his principal statements concerns the opposition between the "raw" (nature) and the "cooked" (culture): *Le Cru et le cuit* (Paris: Plon, 1964); translated into English by John and Doreen Weightman as *The Raw and the Cooked* (New York: Harper & Row, 1969). See also the interpretation of William Faulkner's *Go Down, Moses* by Wesley Morris in *Friday's Footprint: Structuralism and the Articulated Text* (Columbus: Ohio State University Press, 1979), pt. 1, "The Pilgrimage of Being."

no tiene nuestra sensibilidad. No se dan cuenta de lo que les pasa. ¡Y tal vez no convenga del todo que se den cuenta. Yo no encuentro ningún argumento razonable para refutar esa mentira injusta.
No puedo hacer otra cosa que decirles:
—Es mentira. Mentira que inventaron ustedes los ricos para quedarse tranquilos. ¡Pero es mentira!
Si me preguntan por qué, yo tendría solamente algo que decirles, muy poca cosa. Sería esto
—¡Yo he visto llorar a los humildes y no de dolor, que de dolor lloran hasta los animales!
¡Y por agradecimiento, por agradecimiento sí que no saben llorar los ricos! (p. 163)

(I have often heard from the lips of the "upper classes," as they are accustomed to call themselves, things like these: "Do not worry so much about your *descamisados*. That kind of person does not have our sensitivity. They do not understand what happens to them. And perhaps it is better on the whole that they do not."
I can find no reasonable argument with which to refute this unjust lie.
I can do nothing but tell them:
"It's a lie. A lie you, the rich, invented yourselves, so as not to be troubled. But it's a lie."
If they asked me why, I would have only one thing to tell them, very little. It would be this:
"I have seen the humble cry, but not from pain, for even animals cry from pain! I have seen them cry out of gratefulness!
And out of gratefulness, the rich, indeed, do not know how to cry.) (p. 110)

Although not developed in any systematic fashion, the patterns of binary opposition in *Razón* between corrupt, artificial culture and innocent, spontaneous nature are extensive. In addition to intuition versus disingenuous mediocrity (see chapter 14, "¿Intuición?"), *descamisados* versus oligarchy, sincerity versus cynicism, there are several eulogies of radical spontaneity versus disinterested methodicalness. Ironically foreshadowing how Eva's frenetic activities contributed to breaking her fragile health, *Razón* speaks over and over again of her marathon campaigns, her chidings by Perón for her long absences from his side, her late hours, and so on. One photograph, showing her waving from her car under a belltower whose clock marks 5:40—presumably a.m. because of the darkness—has subsequently been widely circulated on the covers of the album and published text of Weber's musical *Evita*.[11] *Razón*, despite the constant reminders that Eva's activities are only an extension of Perón's political and social programs, runs the risk of praising Eva's intense spontaneity at the expense of Perón's rational calculations. The following page, from chapter 44, "Cómo me pagan el pueblo y Perón," is typical of the encomium of free-wheeling disorder:

> Además yo he sido siempre desordenada en mi manera de hacer las cosas; me gusta el "desorden" como si el desorden fuese mi medio normal de vida. Creo que nací para la Revolución. He vivido siempre en libertad. Como los pájaros, siempre me gustó el aire libre del bosque. Ni siquiera he podido tolerar esa cierta esclavitud que es la vida en la casa paterna, o la vida en el pueblo natal. . . . Muy temprano en mi vida dejé mi hogar y mi pueblo, y desde entonces siempre he sido libre. He querido vivir por mi cuenta y he vivido por mi cuenta.
>
> Por eso no podré jamás ser funcionario, que es atarse a un sistema, encadenarse a la gran máquina del Estado y cumplir allí todos los días una función determinada.
>
> No. Yo quiero seguir siendo pájaro suelto en el bosque inmenso.
>
> Me gusta la libertad como le gusta al pueblo, y en eso como en ninguna otra cosa me reconozco *pueblo*. (p. 243)

(Also, I have always been disorderly in my way of doing things; I like disorder as though it were my normal way of life. I think I was born for the revolution. I have always lived at liberty. Like the birds, I have always liked the fresh air of the woods. I was not even able to tolerate that degree of servitude which is part of life in one's parents' home or the life of one's home town. Very early in life I left my home and my town and since then I have always been free. I have wished to live on my own, and I have lived on my own.

That is why I could never be a functionary, which means being tied to a system, chained to the great machine of State and fulfilling a definite function there every day.

No. I want to continue to be a bird, free in an immense forest.

I enjoy liberty as the people enjoy it, and in that, more than anything else, I recognize that I am completely of the people.) (pp. 163–64)

The narrator of *Razón* offers what purports to be a unique conception of political activism, rather than any particular version of events alluded to. This eschewal of the hoary model of the

11. Andrew Lloyd Weber and Tim Rice, *Evita: The Legend of Evita Perón (1919–1952)*. The Weber-Rice musical inspired James W. Wilkie and Monica Menell-Kinberg to examine various sources and versions of the material in their "*Evita*: From Elitelore to Folklore."

"insider's story" in favor of a special mode of self-conception is the basis of the narrative's appeal to the reader and the privileged character of her persona.

III

One of the rhetorical ploys used by the narrator of *Razón* is to speak of dramatic roles and to oppose artificial theatricality with the authenticity of her spontaneous vitalism. The most significant use of this ploy in *Razón* is in chapter 16, "Eva Perón and Evita," followed by chapter 17, "Evita." Running a little less than four pages, chapter 16 sets forth the disjunction between the wife of the president as defined by the protocols of Argentine tradition and the wife of the supreme leader of Peronismo as defined by the privileged mission she has been called upon to fulfill. This chapter indicates both the rhetoric of *Razón* and the terms with which the narrator posits the antitheses that justify the uniqueness of her discourse:

> Pude ser una mujer de Presidente como lo fueron otras.
> Es un papel sencillo y agradable: trabajo de los días de fiesta, trabajo de recibir honores, de "engalanarse" para representar según un protocolo que es casi lo mismo que pude hacer antes, y creo que más o menos bien, en el teatro o en el cine. . . .
> La verdad es otra: yo, que había aprendido de Perón a elegir caminos poco frecuentados, no quise seguir el antiguo modelo de esposa de Presidente. . . .
> No nací para eso. Por el contrario, siempre hubo en mi alma un franco repudio para con "esa clase de teatro".
> Pero además, yo no era solamente la esposa del Presidente de la República, era también la mujer del conductor de los argentinos.
> A la doble personalidad de Perón debía corresponder una doble personalidad en mí: una, la de Eva Perón, mujer del Presidente, cuyo trabajo es sencillo y agradable, trabajo de los días de fiesta, de recibir honores, de funciones de gala; u otra, la de Evita, mujer del Líder de un pueblo que ha depositado en él toda su fe, toda su esperanza y todo su amor.
> Unos pocos días al año, represento el papel de Eva Perón; en ese papel creo que me desempeño cada vez mejor, pues no me parece difícil ni desagradable.
> La inmensa mayoría de los días soy en cambio Evita, puente tendido entre las esperanzas del pueblo y las manos realizadoras de Perón, primera peronista argentina, y éste sí que me resulta papel difícil, y en el que nunca estoy totalmente contenta de mí. (pp. 85–88)

(I might have been a President's wife like the others. It is a simple and agreeable role: a holiday job, the task of receiving honors, of decking oneself out to go through the motions prescribed by social dictates. It is all very similar to what I was able to do previously, and I think more or less successfully, in the theater and in the cinema. . . . The truth is different. I, who had learned from Perón to choose unusual paths, did not wish to follow the old pattern of wife of the President. . . . I was not born for that. On the contrary, there was always in my soul an open repugnance for that kind of acting.

But also, I was not only the wife of the President of the Republic, I was also the wife of the Leader of the Argentines. I had to have a double personality to correspond with Perón's double personality. One, Eva Perón, wife of the President, whose work is simple and agreeable, a holiday job of receiving honors, of gala performances; the other "Evita," wife of the Leader of a people who have placed all their faith in him, all their hope and all their love.

A few days of the year I act the part of Eva Perón; and I think I do better each time in that part, for it seems to me to be neither difficult nor disagreeable.

The immense majority of days I am, on the other hand, "Evita," a link stretched between the hopes of the people and the fulfilling hands of Perón, Argentina's first woman Peronista—and this indeed is a difficult role for me, and one in which I am never quite satisfied with myself.) (pp. 57–59)

The oppositions here are clearly set forth.

The following chapter then develops further the figure of Evita and her unique role. There is no particular subtlety either in this disjunctive scheme or in its textual elaboration: *Razón*, as a document directed toward a popular audience, uses the most overt strategies of signification. It also repudiates any pretense at the sort of concentrated articulation that provides the "pleasure of the text" for the reader of high literature. Indeed, the dominant figure of diction in Eva Perón's book is the disjunctive formula "not A, but [rather] B," a stylistic device that unambiguously specifies what is to be valued by explicitly juxtaposing it with what is to be repudiated. Two examples of this procedure in the chapter I have just quoted will suffice: "Nunca la oligarquía fué hostil . . . [not A] / La verdad es otra . . . [but rather B]." "No nací para eso. [not A] / Por el contrario . . . [but rather B]."

No text is free of rhetoric, and the most unpretentious forms of discourse are characterized by commonplace rhetorical formulas that, because of their frequency in our everyday speech, seem natural. Without entering into a thorough analysis of the stylistic features of *Razón*, we may say that its forms of verbal expression fluctuate between the automatic devices of everyday speech and the crowd-arousing bombast that typified the political addresses of both of the Peróns. One such device, which precedes the two examples of disjunctive listing I have quoted, is the series of three rhetorical questions in which Eva wonders why the oligarchy cannot accept her. (There is a disingenuous candidness about *Razón*, as Eva zeroes in on all of her traits that so infuriated the opposition; the only notable ones she "overlooks" are her reputed past as a prostitute-courtesan and her rough-hewn accent and grammar.)

A functional irony underlies *Razón*, and I use the phenomenological qualifier to avoid the intentional fallacy of ascribing this irony to the conscious strategies of the author. This irony concerns the overlapping images of the narrator as self-effacing and the narrator as the lone figure on the stage of her own drama. The self-effacement of the narrative persona combines feminine demureness ("We women can't always understand the complexity of things"; "A woman only thinks with her heart"), devotion to Perón ("What I am I owe to Perón"; "What I am doing is only to enhance Perón and his programs"; "To understand me is to understand Perón"), and the repeated desire to go down in history not as an important political figure in her own right but as an effective instrument of the movement she represents. Characteristically, the narrator speaks of herself in this regard in the third person, as though both Eva and Evita were dissociated from the identity of the narrative voice:

> Quisiera que de ella [Evita] se diga, aunque no fuese más que en una pequeña nota, al pie del capítulo maravilloso que la historia ciertamente dedicará a Perón, algo que fuese más o menos esto:
> "Hubo, al lado de Perón, una mujer que se dedicó a llevarle al Presidente las esperanzas del pueblo, que luego Perón convertía en realidades".
> Y me sentiría debidamente, sobradamente compensada si la nota terminase de esta manera:
> "De aquella mujer sólo sabemos que el pueblo la llamaba, cariñosamente, *Evita*." (p. 95)

> (I would like it to be said of her, even if only in a small footnote to the marvelous chapter which history will certainly devote to Perón, something more or less like this:

"There was, at Perón's side, a woman who dedicated herself to conveying to the President the hopes of the people which later Perón converted into realities." And I would feel duly compensated—and more—if the note ended like this: "All we know about that woman is that the people called her, fondly, *Evita*.") (pp. 63–64)

By contrast, there is hardly a sentence of *Razón* that is not predicate to the *yo* of the narrator.

The dissociation between the first person of the narrator and the portrait of the double personality of Eva-Evita extends also to the interplay between the image of radical innocence projected by the ploys of self-effacement and the image of the Great Woman sharing with her readers her "private knowledge" concerning Perón, his thoughts, and his goals. In many cases, these confidences—the letters Perón sent Eva, sentiments he shared with her, and the emotional turmoils of critical moments like the October 1945 struggle against Perón's incarceration—are typical of the material in women's magazines. On many other occasions, the information shared with the reader summarizes the motives behind the activities of the Peronist couple. In this case the information is not so much new, being a rehash of previously published propaganda and political speeches, as it is emphasized by virtue of the autobiographical context that frames it. The text may use disclaimers to the effect that it is difficult for Evita to describe what went on in Perón's heart, but the entire rationale of *Razón* rests precisely on providing a privileged explanation, through the persona of the narrator, of Perón's and Peronismo's deepest meanings.

IV

I have attempted to demonstrate that the self-alleged uniqueness of Eva Perón's *La razón de mi vida* rests on the dichotomies and binary oppositions that underlie its presentation of Eva's role in her husband's government. This system of oppositions sustains the book's image of Justicialista society in its struggles against what the narrator calls the futility of the past one hundred years of national history (in 1852 the dictator Juan Manuel Rosas was defeated at Caseros, and Argentina began the establishment of a European, liberal society that Peronismo clumsily set out to supersede). The validity of this pattern of oppositions depends, of course, on the assumptions that the reader brings to *Razón.* That is to say, the pattern of oppositions that the narrator establishes from the outset in *Razón* will only be convincing to a reader who accepts the conception of Argentine social history implicit in the book and the explicit references to the events of the 1940s.

The reader must accept the distinction between nature and culture, between *descamisados* and oligarchy (liberal faith would hold that, by personal effort, the humblest citizen can become a wealthy Argentine landowner),[12] between mind and sentiment, between tradition and revolutionary innovation, between, in a word, Eva Perón and her enemies. Only then does *Razón* function as a productive semiotic text, providing an internally reasonable version of certain phenomena and, thereby, justifying the discourse privilege of the feminine narrative persona.

Undoubtedly, it is difficult to read *Razón* in this fashion today. Indeed, *Razón* read in the 1980s invites the same sort of bemused, outraged, condescending readings that befall most of the texts of popular culture in the hands of readers who consider themselves of superior sophistication. *Razón* is without question a document of Argentine popular culture, not because it is the product of the mass industry responsible for national television or women's and sports magazines, but because it was "written" by an author who was addressing herself to a broad-based popular audience and who was in fact a product of the same culture as that audience. It is in this sense that *Razón* must be read within the conventions of popular literature,[13] not so much because it is an inherently puerile text, but because many of its discourse conventions—from the short sentences and paragraphs and the abundant exclamation marks to the high-frequency vocabulary and the rhetorical strategies of the confessional narratives in women's magazines, all supported by a conventional image of sex roles—are inescapably those of the popular culture that still prevails in much of the West.

The American reader insensitive to the values that dominated Argentina during the Peronista period or the Argentine reader

12. One of the paradigmatic liberal interpretations of Argentine history is Henry Stanley Ferns's *Argentina* (London: Benn, 1979).
13. Concerning the conventions for reading popular literature, see the important theoretical statement by James Mellard, "Prolegomena to a Study of the Popular Mode in Narrative." One of the major researchers on Spanish-language popular literature and its scholarly analysis is Andrés Amorós; see his *Subliteraturas.*

either disdainful of or disillusioned with the myths of the Peróns cannot help but read *La razón de mi vida* as self-serving, as intellectually and emotionally dishonest, and as a superb example of literary kitsch. Moreover, it is unlikely that even supporters of Peronismo, like the poet and novelist Leopoldo Marechal, were able to read Eva Perón's book as innocent poetry. Nevertheless, there is a semiotic coherence underlying *Razón*, supported by the narrative persona who appeals to the reader's interest in well-defined terms. Whether the image of a woman's privileged access to a position of powerful political influence is accurate or not is less important than the internal coherence of her narrative. Read on its own terms as either a serious political statement or a "fictional narrative" artfully designed to strike responsive chords in a sympathetic audience, *Razón* deserves its important role as an eloquent example of the literature produced by popular Peronista culture.[14]

14. Significantly, Joseph R. Barager includes a segment from *Razón* in his collection of historical documents relating to Peronismo: *Why Perón Came to Power; The Background to Peronismo in Argentina*, pp. 203–5.

3. The Demythification of Buenos Aires in the Argentine Novel of the Seventies

"The Black Artist's role in America is to aid in the destruction of America as he knows it." LeRoi Jones[1]

"Y aquí es donde la cosa deja de ser como en los avisos." Papá de Mafalda.[2]

("And this is where things cease to be like in the ads.")

I

Any extensive national literary tradition will necessarily manifest at different times, undoubtedly as reactions to earlier works and as responses to specific sociocultural conditions, examples of patriotic phenomena. Aside from the theory that literature can only truly exist when it is either mythificational (functioning to praise or sanctify) or demythificational (serving to deny the validity of cultural referents), and never when it is simply representational, a particular movement within a tradition may manifest itself as demythificational in response to its immediate literary antecessors.[3] To a certain extent, such a situation obtains in the Latin American novel of the sixties.

Although the works of the *nueva narrativa latinoamericana*, of the "boom," were certainly neither patriotic nor characterized by optimism toward the future of Latin America, many of them were written under the combined influence of the Alianza para el Progreso (President Kennedy's Alliance for Progress) and struggles like that of the Uruguayan left-wing Tupamaros for continental liberation and project, as a consequence, a strong,

1. As quoted by Jerome Klinkowitz, *Literary Disruptions*, p. 104.
2. Quino, *Mafalda 6* (Buenos Aires: Ediciones de la Flor, 1970), no pagination.
3. Concerning rupture as an evolutionary literary process, see Noé Jitrik, "Destrucción de formas en las narraciones," in César Fernández Moreno, ed., *América en su literatura* (Mexico City: Siglo XXI, 1972), pp. 219–42.

positive image of the Latin American experience. In this sense, works like Gabriel García Márquez's *Cien años de soledad* (1967; a novel on the destruction of the cycles of feudal oppression); José Lezama Lima's *Paradiso* (1966; an examination of the artistic liberation of the individual); Carlos Fuentes's *Cambio de piel* (1967; a depiction of the response of natives to the sterile values of bourgeois swingers); Julio Cortázar's *El libro de Manuel* (1973; a revolutionary baby-book for the new generation); Guillermo Cabrera Infante's *Tres tristes tigres* (1967; a description of the *Gotterdämmerung* of the old Havana) are all "positive" vis-à-vis the texture of Latin American experience. They are positive in the sense that they project or imply the bases for political, cultural, and ethical renewal. Although there exists alongside them a series of essentially negative works—the heirs of existentialism and the parricidal movements of the 1950s—the works referred to may be seen as proposing symbolic myths for a new Latin America.[4]

In the case of Argentine literature, we may discern a clear pattern of works that alternate mythificational with demythificational processes of viewing the national experience. There is a discernible demythificational pattern beginning with the earliest examples of national literature: Esteban Echeverría's *El matadero* (circa 1839; an examination of Rosas's Buenos Aires as an enormous, bloody slaughterhouse); José Mármol's *Amalia* (1851–1855; one of the first Gothic romances of good versus evil in Latin America, with the latter incarnate in Rosas triumphant); Eugenio Cambaceres's *Sin rumbo* (1885) and *En la sangre* (1887; naturalistic novels dealing with Creole abulia and immigrant "bad seeds," respectively); Roberto Arlt's *Los siete locos* (1929; a depiction of current Argentine society as a merry-go-round of hopeless weirdos); Ernesto Sabato's *Sobre héroes y tumbas* (1962; a description of the messy backside of the tapestry of Argentine official history); Julio Cortázar's *Rayuela* (1963; a *grande bouffe* of Argentine existentialism and the Buenos Aires–Paris cultural syndrome).

On the other hand, great mythificational works have not been as abundant (I exclude official literature that does not enjoy out-

4. This is the sense of the interviews conducted by Gunter Lorenz in the sixties: *Diálogo con América latina*. See also the essays originally published by Carlos Fuentes in the review *Siempre* and republished in *La nueva novela hispanoamericana*. A revisionist, "denunciatory" perspective is offered by Hernán Vidal, *Literatura hispanoamericana e ideología liberal: surgimiento y crisis (una problemática sobre la dependencia en torno a la narrativa del boom)*.

standing critical endorsement): José Hernández's *Martín Fierro* (1872 and 1879; although it begins as a great anti-establishment denunciation of the treatment of the gaucho, this work concludes with the latter's integration into the new liberal society and has become the official paragon of Argentine literature); Ricardo Güiraldes's *Don Segundo Sombra* (1926; although not specifically urban oriented, the novel concerns the education of the sophisticated citizen-to-be in the meaning of the land); Manuel Mujica Láinez's *Aquí vivieron* (1949; a nostalgic evocation of Creole and oligarchic roots); Leopoldo Marechal's *Adán Buenosayres* (1948; a *porteño Ulysses* and a vanguard *Bildungsroman* on the modern urban citizen).

To be sure, there are numerous other important works that could be mentioned in this regard, and one might easily fall into taxonomic diversions, especially since a good number of works are semantically ambivalent as concerns the issue of mythification and demythification. No matter how much critics of the two extremes of the ideological spectrum (the intense nationalists versus the internationally committed) may believe that literature is ultimately sociopolitically responsive, a large number of Argentine works can only with a great amount of critical overreading be aligned with the controversies concerning mythification and demythification. Indeed, there are works that implicitly deny the validity of such processes and that call for an end to myth; one example would be Guillermo Gentile's *Hablemos a calzón quitado*, a play that decries both guerrilla and bourgeois posturing.

Yet the theoretical models that underpin this study maintain that myth, when viewed as a symbolic narrative in response to a concrete reality that can never be represented directly or without mediation, is a neutral phenomenon.[5] In this sense, all texts are myths. It is only in terms of the intertextuality between verbal texts and larger cultural "texts" (social, cultural, political, ethical, linguistic, and other codes) that we can speak of "mythification" or "demythification." For example, from one perspective one may speak of a process of demythification in García Márquez's *Cien años de soledad*,[6] seeing the novel as an elaborate eschatological vision of Latin America, the end of the

---

5. This position has been maintained most articulately by Brazilians Luiz Costa Lima (*A metamorfose do silêncio* and *A perversão do trapezista*) and Roberto Reis ("A significância ou o resgate da significação").

6. This is the sense of Josefina Ludmer's *Cien años de soledad: una interpretación* (Buenos Aires: Tiempo Contemporáneo, 1972).

cyclical process of feudal repression that destroys both Macondo and the prophetic text itself. Yet reading the novel from a perspective that stresses the symbolic manifestation of cyclical repression, one notes a pattern of demythification based on exaggeration, inversion, and disproportion. In terms of the costumbristic-realistic intertexts, the novel is a "disappointment" in that it does not fulfill the patterns demanded by the intertextual models. In turn, the ways in which those patterns are not fulfilled constitute both the humorousness of the text and its essential demythificational nature. The semantic "distance" between García Márquez's novel of Colombia and the narratives of the indulgently ironic writers of the nineteenth century (for example, Tomás Carrasquilla) is one of the major semiological processes associated with *Cien años de soledad*.

In the case of Mario Vargas Llosa's *La ciudad y los perros* (1963), there was no overwhelming need for the novel, in order to make its point concerning the inherent brutality of the "military way of life" and the homologies between the military ethos and the patterns of civilian society, to make specific references to Lima and to the Colegio Leoncio Prado. Thus, by portraying a value system with sufficient rhetorical strategies to ensure its repudiation, the novel also repudiates a specific range of Latin American reality identified by name. The fact that the process of repudiation is elaborated through reference to a socially vaunted Latin American institution only increases the effectiveness of the demythificational process. Indeed, the incineration of copies of the novel at the Colegio Leoncio Prado when they arrived in Lima from Barcelona, as chilling as it was to the freedom of expression in Peru, was far from a know-nothing overreaction: it may be seen, in fact, as a "critical" response based on a perfectly reasonable and competent reading of the novel.

II

Any study of demythificational structures in Argentine literature must begin with the works of Enrique Medina.[7] Other Argentine writers of the late sixties and early seventies, such as

7. See the entry by Stephen T. Clinton on Medina in David William Foster, ed., *A Dictionary of Contemporary Latin American Authors*, pp. 65–66. Medina's work is also studied by Juan F. Bazán, in his *Narrativa paraguaya y latinoamericana*, pp. 259–73; and by Bella Jozef, "Enrique Medina, o tempo sem recuperação," in her *O jogo mágico*, pp. 118–20.

Manuel Puig, may have attracted a more extensive reception abroad. Nevertheless, Medina's *Las tumbas* (1972)—an essentially autobiographical account of his years in the infamous juvenile corrections center in Buenos Aires whose inauspicious popular name gives the work its title—was the largest-selling title of the seventies in Argentina (over two dozen printings thus far), notwithstanding the serious problems of censorship that it experienced.[8] Medina has produced almost a dozen works in as many years, and all have received extensive critical acclaim. Despite the all-too-justified horror of "right-thinking" Argentine readers, who see in Medina's works a relentless inversion of hallowed myths, Medina's fiction has received favorable reviews in all the literary supplements of Buenos Aires.

However, Medina has been, like the more mainline Puig (mainline because he has enjoyed the full benefits of living in New York City in contact with the American literary establishment), extremely inventive in expanding the staid definitions of "Literature" that prevail in academic and journalistic quarters. Medina has done so primarily by assimilating into a nuclear, symbolically fictional text (and, hence, one that cannot be confused with social-science documentaries) a variety of paraliterary and subliterary phenomena. These phenomena include journalistic modalities, soap-opera strategies for plot ecphrasis, gritty and debased commercial or advertising language, the purple rhetoric of pornography, and the exploitative formulas of more public if not more spiritually enobling girlie magazines. As a result, in terms of normative points of reference for Argentine literature within the official liberal tradition of literature and art as spiritually uplifting, Medina's works are aggressive gestures directed at socially complacent readers. Even the reader who accepts Medina's cultural postulates cannot be truly said to "enjoy" reading one of Medina's novels, so trenchant are they in their aggressive destruction of national myths as represented in the purportedly sophisticated and urban Buenos Aires.[9]

8. See the article by Stephen T. Clinton, "Censorship, Human Rights under Videla."
9. It should be remembered that the repudiation of fiction written by writers like Medina parallels the experience fifty years ago of Roberto Arlt. Arlt attempted to defend himself against the principle charges—sloppy writing, degrading characters and sentiments, abominable style, and ignoble language—in his "Palabras del autor," the prologue to his 1931 *Los lanzallamas*; see his *Obras completas* (Buenos Aires: Compañía General Fabril, 1963), 2:9–11. The is-

Medina's *Strip-tease* is one of the most audacious novels of recent Argentine fiction.[10] It is also one of the most eloquent—and probably one of the most "constructively repugnant"—examples of using megapolitan Buenos Aires for demythifying Argentine culture. *Strip-tease* may be approached in terms of a number of significant organizing principles. In the first place, the novel exemplifies the grimy language of the urban underbelly of Buenos Aires that is one of Medina's abiding hallmarks. Superficially, this language is documentarily accurate in its precise transcription of recurring taboo words, in the metaphors and rhetorical turns of speech characteristic of a specific sociocultural stratum, and in the various discourse patterns associated with that stratum.

Yet no work of fiction is strictly speaking documentary, and *Strip-tease* is recognizable as fiction in part because of the degree to which its backs off from being rigorously documentary. As a consequence, we may say that the language in *Strip-tease* functions not just as a means of recording accurately a particularly unappealing group of individuals and their way of life but also as an especially effective—if not downright risky—way of establishing a narrative contract with the reader. The latter is surely to be repulsed by what is described in *Strip-tease* and even more by how it is described. The following segment may be read as high camp in its clear echoing of the worst prose of parapornographic fiction. But it can hardly be said to invite the reader to enter into and identify with the world being portrayed through the stage spectacle that we see the protagonist witnessing:

sues involved are reviewed in perspective by Juan Carlos Ghiano, "Los personajes de Arlt," in his *Testimonio de la novela argentina* (Buenos Aires: Leviatán, 1956), pp. 169–84. Arlt was not given as bad a time by the critics as he liked to pretend, and it is only fair to note that Medina has also enjoyed considerable support from significant segments of the Argentine critical establishment.

10. Buenos Aires: Ediciones Corregidor, 1976. These comments are an expanded version of "Bare Words and Naked Truths," *The American Hispanist*, no. 12 (1976):17–19. As should be immediately apparent, this is not a semiotic study, nor should it pretend to be one. Semiology—or semiotics—is not to be confused with literary criticism. They are separate academic or intellectual disciplines. Literary analysis, however, may properly be informed by semiological concepts, as it may be by Freudian psychology, Marxism, or linguistics. Thus, a semiological analysis of the narrative structures of the novels studied in this chapter would look quite different from the analyses I offer and yet would not necessarily constitute literary criticism. Concerning the intersection of semiology and literary criticism, see Terence Hawkes, *Structuralism and Semiotics* (Berkeley: University of California Press, 1977).

Se acerca hasta el mismo borde y esto me permite olerle el sudor a zorra que le corre por todo el cuerpacho, flor de despacho. ¡¡¡Yo estoy en mi mejor momento!!!. . . ¡¡¡El momento de la verdad!!!. . . ¡¡¡Sigo ya automáticamente con el estilo tirabuzón de masturbarme!!!. . . ¡¡¡Tengo los brazos dormidos!!!. . . ¡¡¡Ya ni sé cuál es el que estoy usando!!!. . . ¡¡¡No me importa!!!. . . ¡¡¡Sé que esta carrera es mía!!!. . . ¡¡¡Y juré que la ganaba!!!. . . ¡¡¡La lengua ya la tengo por el cinturón!!!. . . ¡¡¡La Bizca me mira!!!. . . ¡¡¡Me ve en mi verdad, todo desarmado en mi butaca!!!. . . ¡¡¡Nada me importa!!!. . . ¡¡¡Ya no doy más, con los ojos le pido por favor que haga un último esfuerzo!!!. . . ¡¡¡Me ve, con los ojos acuosos yo, con la sonrisa abierta ella; me ve con el língam en la mano, estilo tirabuzón!!!. . . ¡¡¡Se me acerca!!!. . . ¡¡¡La tengo aquí, a un metro de distancia!!!. . . ¡¡¡Solamente tengo que levantar un poco el marote para mirarla, pero está aquí, frente a mí, viéndome abrazado a mi rencor!!!. . .

—Para vos, Pichón. . .

Al pronunciar esas palabras abre sus brazos y deja en libertad dos enormes pedazos de carne blanca con unos pimpollitos hermosos en las puntas. . . ¡¡¡Señor del cielo y de la tierra!!!. . . ¡¡¡AAAaaahhhhh!!!. . . ¡¡¡Muerto soy!!!. . . Y me desparramo en el suelo.[11]

(She comes down to the edge of the stage, allowing me to smell the foxy odor that permeates her whole body, hody hody. I've reached my best moment!!! . . . The moment of truth!!! . . . I'm going full steam jacking off corkscrew style!!! . . . My arms are going to sleep!!! . . . I don't even know which one I'm using now!!! . . . It doesn't matter!!! . . . I know this race belongs to me!!! . . . And I swore I would win it!!! . . . My tongue hangs down to my waist!!! . . . Cross-eyed Beauty is watching me!!! . . . She sees me in my moment of truth, disarmed before the world in my seat!!! . . . Nothing matters to me!!! . . . I can't stand it any more, and my eyes beg her please to make the final effort!!! . . . She sees me, my eyes all runny, her smile wide as her face—she sees me with my cock in my hand, corkscrew style!!! . . . She comes over to me!!! . . .

I have her within reach, just a meter away!!! . . .

All I have to do is to raise my head a little to look at her, but here she is, right in front of me, seeing me hugging my bitterness!!! . . .

"This one's for you, kid . . ."

As she says these words, she opens her arms and sets free two enormous mountains of white flesh with pretty little buttons on the tips . . . God in heaven and earth!!! . . . AAAaaahhhhh!!! . . . I've died and gone to heaven!!! . . . And I come all over the floor.)

---

11. *Strip-Tease*, pp. 196–97. Further citations will be made by page number in the text.

The repugnant texture of such language—that is, the verbalizations of the narrator-protagonist and not the debased literary style of the author—serves as a challenge to the reader. On the one hand, it challenges the reader to "take it as it is," despite whatever preconceived ideas the reader may hold concerning the nature of human commerce. On the other hand, such language is an open threat to the reader's spiritual ability to persevere in the reading of the novel: by assaulting so trenchantly the reader's presumed linguistic—and, thereby, emotional—taboos, the novel becomes a gauge of the reader's ability and willingness to "take it straight." This is called "writing without concessions," and it is an important element of the narrative contract in many Latin American novels, although seldom as starkly as in Medina's works.[12] There are few social taboos as rigid as those that control language registers, both in dictating what is to be considered elegant and ennobling language and in proscribing what is to be considered depraved expression. By seeming to sink to the latter, by eschewing the former, and by failing to appeal to a hypothetical "average" colloquial norm, Medina's novel creates a range of narrative language that is demythificational in its assaultive threat to the implied "right-thinking" reader.[13]

In addition to stating the rules for its own linguistic register vis-à-vis an ideal reader, this sort of language becomes semantically functional through the range of societal taboos portrayed with graphic eloquence. Thus, references to sexual practices offend Argentine primness in both vocabulary and referents. It is noteworthy that the novel concerns heterosexual drives presented as the grotesque and therefore natural extensions of acceptable sexuality. In this way the novel manages to be as repugnant to alleged good taste as it would be if explicit homosexuality were involved in the manner of William Burroughs or John Rechy. The grotesque extensions of "normal" sexuality lie

12. For a discussion of reader contracts and other issues associated with discourse models of literature, see Mary Louise Pratt, *Toward a Speech Act Theory of Literary Discourse.*

13. An abundance of material exists on "obscenity" in contemporary literature. One sourcebook is Eleanor Widmer, ed., *Freedom and Culture: Literary Censorship in the 70s* (Belmont, Calif.: Wadsworth, 1970). See also David Lott, *The Erotic in Literature; A Historical Survey of Pornography* (New York: Julian Messner, 1961). To the best of my knowledge, the subject has not been treated with respect to Latin American literature. Also of interest is Felice Flanery Lewis's chapter "Four-Letter Words and American Literature," in her *Literature, Obscenity, & Law* (Carbondale: Southern Illinois University Press, 1976), pp. 134–60.

not in the narrative's proposal of imagined activities but in its clinical contemplation and treatment of sociologically recognizable extensions of the patterns of heterosexual behavior.

The grotesqueness also derives from the means by which sex is contextualized in the novel: the raunchy striptease parlors and shows, the desperate individuals who seek sexual gratification in the masturbatory contemplation of a remote object of fantastic desire and an array of attendant secret fetishisms, the exploitation of sex for commercial and assorted venial reasons, the way in which the patrons of seedy burlesque houses fall prey to psychotically disturbed perverts, the degradation of the "performers" who not only must put their flesh on parade in the tradition of the trite beauty pageant but also are obliged to see it deteriorate until it becomes the object of unrestrained scorn by the "fans." These are all specifically thematic elements that could be detailed in terms of the social, cultural, and political contexts of the novel, but they attain a specifically fictive value in their rendition through the overall linguistic framework. Far from any pornographic voyeurism, all that is possible from any but the most callous of readers is a disgusted repudiation of the entire system of values that the novel evokes. These values are implicit (society at large) as well as explicit (the seedy shows that replay structures of society in grotesquely accurate registers).

In short, the fictional search for sexual initiation and fulfillment in the striptease shows of Buenos Aires by a young man from the provinces is presented in such a way that the primal urge of sex becomes a revolting phenomenon. Neither joyous libidinousness nor ribald scatology has any place in the world that Medina's characters and their desires inhabit—nor in the narrative discourse that seeks to represent them for us.

Aside from the specifically dramatic use of language as an instrument for attacking accepted societal values, we may refer also to the image of Buenos Aires projected by the striptease microcosm that Medina's novel presents. It is clear that Medina's work concerns a marginal society whose values are degenerate when compared with an implicit norm for human dignity. Otherwise seemingly "solid" citizens are attracted to this spectrum of depravity in an eloquent violation of the public standards to which they may claim to adhere. This is a particularly effective form of demythification, to the extent that a particular social class is portrayed as behaving in a fashion explicitly belying its general criteria for social normalcy and decency. That is, the characters of *Strip-tease*, while not all pillars of society—indeed, the majority are quite marginal—are not the criminal and psychopathic dregs of society. Rather, they are "regular" individuals attracted to the striptease spectacle for highly personal reasons having to do with their individual psychological existences within a particular social and cultural context. In terms of the novel's narrative texture, the striptease phenomenon functions as a uniquely grotesque cluster of signs that, in addition to the moral and spiritual issues it raises, serves to signify, in the lives of the individuals affected, a necessary if unconfessable deviation from the respectable norms of the world they inhabit outside the show places.

In this regard, it should be stressed that Medina's novel does not denounce sex or any specific manifestations of sexual desire and release. Rather, the scathing denunciation that the novel projects arises from the focus on certain manifestations of sexual behavior as the only available outlets for normal sexual passion in a repressive society. The irony arises specifically from the way in which the ethos of the striptease parlors unwittingly mimics the clichés and stereotyped values of the society in which it functions as a grotesque alternative. The novel postulates not two opposing systems of values, but one system that contains its own elements of semiological rupture. From one point of view, the characters are drawn to the striptease because it offers them an opportunity to express sexual drives proscribed by society at large. From another point of view, normal sexual desire must be channeled in degraded and degrading forms because society at large will only allow such forms: sex apart from the repressed expression approved by the prevailing moral and social standards must, by definition, be degrading, a circumstance that can be argued to engender, in turn, degraded sexual drives. Medina's novel consists, to a large measure, of various elaborations of this line of thinking.

There is, then, in Medina's novel a concerted attempt to reveal a hidden and hideous face of Argentine cultural values, the painted mask of sinister desire beneath the well-scrubbed mien of the innocent chorine of the tourist's Argentina. This interplay is reinforced paratextually by the contrast between the kittenishly alluring face on the back cover and the diabolic harlot's visage that adorns the front cover; it involves innocent versus corrupt flesh, the image of cover girl versus the graphic stamp of iniquitous sin, acceptable seductiveness (as institutionalized in feminine fashion) versus unmentionable depravities. These are some of the binary oppositions that *Striptease* marshals in its antimythificational image of Argentine society. The narrative is presented by a first-person narrator, a provincial youth whose "discovery" of Buenos Aires is replicated in the reader's discovery of the novel: both are engaged in varieties of reading, interpretation, and assimilation. This is why language is so important in *Strip-tease*. Language becomes degraded—that is, it deviates from the neutrally acceptable journalistic norm that Western society maintains as a *stylus mediocris*—as the protagonist plumbs ever more deeply the demimonde of the striptease show. Like those psychiatrists who study defective linguistic performance as an objective correlative of mental dysfunctions,[14] Medina utilizes debased linguistic expression to signify the absolute depravation of the striptease habitués and the growing spiritual disintegration of the narrator-initiate. Thus, as he is transformed from an innocent if frustrated provincial to a communicant fully indoctrinated into the mysteries of the secret cult that he adopts as the true expression of his being (only to look forward to dying of a heart attack as a seedy old man while masturbating in the presence of a gyrating fifty-year-old *vedette*), the narrator's language decays accordingly, ending in only a gurgle (see pp. 519–20).

Degradation of language ultimately becomes linguistic disintegration, best exemplified in the long section on masturbatory techniques that is part of the initiation into the confraternity of striptease votaries:

> PARAGUITA. Tradicional estilo de p. . . argentino. Q. . . . . es e. más j. . . . . . de t. . . . los e. . . . . . dentro d. la c. . . . . Es m. . indicado p. . . entablar g. . . . . amistades o t. . . . tertulias a. . . . . Es m. . similar a. estilo t. . . . . . .: se c. . . . la c. . . . . . . con l. palma de la m. . . y s. apoyan l. . cinco d. . . . . . en e. fibroso c. . . . con v. . . . . ., con e. ritmo y. . uno d. . . . se s. . . y s. baja l. mano, l. . . . . . . de e. . . manera y. . el c. . . . . se h. . . hombre. E. muy c. . . . entre l. . barritas d. pibes c. . . . . juegan a ver a quién l. salta p. . . . . . También s. le l. . . . en

14. This is the line of research pursued in Argentina by David Liberman and David Maldavsky, *Psicoanálisis y semiótica: sentidos de realidad y categorizaciones estilísticas* (Buenos Aires: Paidós, 1975).

a. . . . . . comarcas e. . . . . Vergonzoso d. . . . . a q. . se e. . . . . .
el e. . . . . . vital y móvil. E. el p. . . . . de l. . elegantes d. . . .
de s. . . . . . . cuando v. . al c. . . solas. . . S. origen e. profunda-
mente r. . . . . . . y s. han h. . . . . . interesantes t. . . . . . en l. .
jeroglíficos e. . . . . . y m. . . . . Es e. más r. . . . . para
d. . . . . de l. . comidas p. . . . . no c. . . . la d. . . . . . . (Pp.
146–47)

(THE UMBRELLA. Traditional Argentine style of . . . [What follows is an elliptic description of this "style." Since it is elliptic, any
attempt at translation would be essentially a spurious text based on
what one guesses the missing words represent.])

In this sense the novel is exceptionally successful in using
the subversion of language as a semiological process that gives
form to the novel's subversion in terms of a thematics of social
denunciation, of a particular structure of values. Note should
also be taken of the incorporation—and deformation—of words
and phrases from "prestige" foreign languages (for example,
the title itself); this is also a significant aspect of the novel's response to a specifically Buenos Aires milieu.

Finally, Medina's novel is particularly striking as a black *Divine Comedy*. This is yet one more facet of its strategies for demythification. Intertextually, the novelist has adopted the narrative plan, specific details, and the appropriately inverted
eschatological design of Dante's poem. The young innocent at a
turning point in his life; the descent into a nether world (most
of the striptease parlors are belowground); the presence of
the helpful and thoroughly knowledgeable Virgilian guide;
the quest for an ideal almost beyond reach (the Beatrice-like
vedettes); the contemplation of the human condition as it affects
and afflicts one's fellow travelers; the first-person narrative "I"
as the voice of an appalling, repugnant, pathetic Everyman figure: these are all features of an inverted accommodation of one
of the great masterpieces of the official culture of the West. Indeed, the reader will recognize with little effort the intertextuality between *Strip-tease* and the *Divine Comedy*. The fact that
the narrator remains mired in a mundane Inferno, with the as-
cent toward any redeeming transcendence precluded, is the
single most important element of demythification in the novel:
Buenos Aires as a debauched striptease parlor is a dead-end Inferno with no spiritual salvation possible.

III

Many contemporary Argentine fabulators may be considered direct heirs to Roberto Arlt's implacable anatomies of the Buenos Aires underbelly, but none of the standardbearers has attracted greater attention than Medina. He replaces Arlt's expressionistic whimsy and existential malaise with a novelistic equivalent of the theater of cruelty. Arlt's writing was complemented by the more somber social realists, who sought to engage our sympathy for the trammeled underdog via a series of rhetorical processes that defined the world in terms of the bad oppressors and the good oppressed. By contrast, Medina disturbs the reader profoundly through his rejection of these processes, and his characters and their experiences (even quasi-autobiographical ones) are repulsive as part of a strategy for emphasizing the degree of social degradation they are unwillingly obliged to endure. Norman Mailer and James Baldwin at their harshest come close in American fiction to the texture of Medina's demythification, while Gore Vidal and William Burroughs use calculatedly precise images of the worst of our sociocultural myths to induce in us the same degree of revulsion (although less known, Herbert Selby also comes close to competing with the range of horror in Medina's novels).

Perros de la noche is particularly effective in this regard because of its image of how a woman, specifically the unreflective woman of the laboring classes, is quite literally "trashed" (*basureada* in Argentine Spanish) by the men she is called upon to serve. Mercedes is forced by her brother (for whom she is also a concubine) to support the two of them by taking jobs as a stripteaser and go-go dancer:

—¡Con ustedes la graciosa y sensual Vicky Day!

Y el tanque subió al escenario por detrás del biombo. Ya era hora que le cambiaran la música y probaran otro ritmo porque el género tropical no le iba para nada. Mercedes saltaba exactamente igual que la primera vez que se desnudó en público. Clavaba la vista en un punto fijo y se olvidaba de todo, por eso era que no seguía el ritmo, porque se olvidaba de escucharlo. Pensaba en los bailes del barrio con sus amigas, no le importaba mucho que la mayoría de las veces fuera la única que se quedaba sentada en la mesa, muriéndose por dentro, espiando a Facundo que bailaba con todas las chicas, porque todas querían bailar con él. ¿Qué sería de Facundo? ¿Alguna vez habría pensado en ella como mujer? Todas sus amigas siempre hablaban de la gran vida, de la noche, de los hombres, los whiskys, ellas que solamente tomaban gaseosas, imaginaban que no sería del todo malo tener montones de hombres para elegir. Como ella ahora, que tenía montones de hombres a su disposición. De todas las edades. Algunos respectuosos y otros no. Todo lo que ella deseaba ya lo tenía. Si es que eso era lo que había querido. ¿Qué era lo que más ambicionaba? Un hombre. Mamá. Que la quisiera y la respetara y la acariciara con respeto, no como estos sudorosos que nada sabían de caricias, que lo único que sabían hacer era manosear, pellizcar con esas manos callosas que al solo contacto lastimaban. ¿Eligir? No, en realidad no elegía.[15]

("On stage, the graceful and sensuous Vicky Day!"
The tank climbed up on the stage from behind the screen. It was time for them to change her music and to try some other rhythm—tropical beats were not for her. Mercedes jumped about just as she had the first time she stripped in public. She fixed her gaze on a point in space and forgot about everything, which was why she couldn't follow the beat—she simply forgot to listen to it. She was thinking about the neighborhood dances with her girlfriends. It didn't matter to her that most of the time she was the only one left sitting at the table, dying on the inside, spying on Facundo, who was dancing with all the girls because all of the girls wanted to dance with him. What can have become of Facundo? Did he ever think about her as a woman? Her girlfriends used to talk all the time about the great life, of the night, of men, of whiskey, they who would only drink soda pop used to think it couldn't be all bad to have tons of men to choose from. Like her now, who had tons of men at her beck and call. All ages. Some respectful, others not. Everything she ever wanted she now had. If that's what she wanted. What did she most want? A man. Mama. Someone who would love and respect her and caress her with respect, not like these sweaty oafs who know nothing about caresses. The only thing they knew about was manhandling, pinching her with their horny hands that hurt at the slightest touch. Choose? No, in reality she had no choice.)

Perros is also a striking example of one alternative for feminist literature in Argentina. The novel concerns a dim-witted brother and sister who, upon the death of their sainted and self-sacrificing mother, are left to fend for themselves. The concerns and experiences of this incestuous couple in their mean

---

15. *Perros de la noche*, pp. 97–98. Further citations will be made by page number in the text.

little world constitute a microcosm of all of the spiritual nastiness Medina sees as paradigmatic of Buenos Aires. That their relationship becomes tragically destructive (tragic in the Brechtian sense of detached illustration, achieved through the medium of a relentless narrator) bespeaks Medina's implied proposition that innocence is the unknown handmaiden of man's fall, not his romantic salvation. The relationship between the two protagonists—lover and mistress, manager and "talent" agent, pimp and whore, and, simply, man and woman—is created through narrative combinations and transformations of the patterns that exist between them. Medina's novel is a striking translation of sexism in Latin American society. Like Manuel Puig, Medina finds a reliable image of a degraded and devalued humanity in the traditional man-woman relationships, in the myths of *machomanía*, and in the subtle way in which institutionalized sex is a subcategory of destructive violence. The following passage concludes a long section that describes the "starring" role Mercedes is forced to play in a pornographic movie that stops just short of being a snuff film (the first ones of which, incidentally, were allegedly produced in Argentina); this is one of the key segments of the novel concerning the literal trashing of human beings:

> —Listo. Se terminó.
> —¿Qué tal salió?
> Preguntó el hombre serio, preocupado por los resultados artísticos.
> Como lo soñó el autor. Una pinturita. Creo que ni voy a tener que compaginar nada. Salió todo muy auténtico.
> ¿Y de luz?
> —No se preocupe. Expuse bien. Y mi fotómetro es de los que se usan en Europa, ¡por aquí no se consiguen! Cualquier cosa, manejo la copia en el laboratorio. Por favor, me apagan las luces, ustedes que están cerca.
> Uno de los gorilas se acercó a un tablerito que estaba en el suelo y movió una llave, quedaron iluminados solamente por una lamparita que colgaba del medio del techo. Una vez que los ojos se adaptaron a la nueva luz, el hombre serio, un ser humano al fin, se apiadó de la cosa.
> —A ver si le tiran un poco de agua para que despierte.
> —¡Vamos pardita, arriba! ¡La fiesta terminó!
> El bulto apenas si respondía con algunos espasmos. Al menos respondía. A los mamuts esto no les extrañaba ya que conocían su trabajo y dominaban perfectamente la resistencia de un saco de

papas. La sangre estaba saliendo pausadamente, señal que ya estaba por deternerse. Uno de los gorilas, el que se vistió primero, salió y volvió con un balde de agua. De un golpe Mercedes quedó bañada. Sus ojos pestañaron y el cuerpo, pesadamente, giró al otro lado. Los bestias la levantaron y la sentaron. La cabezota estaba casi desprendida, no había manera de enderezarla. Con un poco de empeño lo consiguieron. ¡La fueron vistiendo! ¡Los monigotes gigantes vestían a Mercedes como a un bebé! Claro que la pobre no tenía la más mínima idea de lo que ocurría. La cargaron y la depositaron en el sofá. En paz quedó acostada esperando a su príncipe azul. Volvió a pensar en la foto de la japonesa. Mamá. (pp. 189–90)

("Great. Wrap it up."
"How'd it come out?"
The question came from the serious man, concerned about artistic results.

Just like the author dreamed it. A picture story. I don't even think I'll have to do any cutting. It came out real authentic.

"What about the light?"
"Not to worry. I shot it well. And my photometer is the kind they use in Europe. You can't even get them here!" If there is any problem, I can work with the copy in the lab. Get the lights for me, will you?, since you're right there.

One of the thugs went over to the control panel on the floor and turned a switch. They were now lit by just a small lamp hanging from the middle of the ceiling. Once their eyes had adapted to this new light, the serious one, a human being after all, took pity on the thing.

"Why don't you throw some water on her? Maybe she'll come to."
"Come on, toots, on your feet! The party's over!"
The sack barely answered with a few spasms. At least there was some sign of life. This came as no surprise to the mammoths, since they knew their job and could handle the weight of a sack of potatoes. Blood was dripping only a little now, a sign that it was about to stop. One of the thugs, the one who got dressed first, went out and came back with a pail of water. Suddenly Mercedes was drenched. Her eyes blinked and her body heavily rolled over to the other side. The goons picked her up and sat her down. Her head was hanging half off and there was no way to make it stay up. With a little effort they managed it. They were dressing her! The giant creeps were dressing Mercedes as though she were a baby! Of course the poor woman hadn't the slightest idea what was going on. They picked her up and deposited her on the sofa. She lay there peacefully waiting for her prince in blue. She thought again about the photograph of the Japanese woman. Mama.)

IV

Although less audaciously structured than Medina's novels, Reina Roffé's fiction provides an excellent example of how contemporary feminist literature, with its emphasis on sex roles (which is an eminently semiological way of viewing interpersonal relationships), occupies a central position within a demythificational tradition.

Literary and media censorship prevailed in Argentina from the midsixties to the end of 1983, eloquent if oblique testimony to seriousness of serious artistic expression in the face of tremendous odds. Particularly disturbing was the rash of prohibitions against works by women writers; these included Griselda Gambaro's *Ganarse la muerte*[16] (Gambaro is one of Latin America's leading playwrights, although she devoted herself to fiction in the late seventies because of the difficulties of theatrical production during the period); Cecilia Absatz's *Féiguele y otras mujeres*[17]; and Reina Roffé's *Monte de Venus*.[18]

Roffé's novel is particularly striking because of its unremitting, iconoclastic vision of Argentine womanhood, and it is not difficult to see why it was banned in Argentina, where open discussion of sex and societal roles can be a dangerous undertaking. Argentina is not an open society when it comes to sexual mores and "alternate" life-styles. Its prudishness has long been a major literary topic, from at least the time of Roberto Arlt's *Los siete locos* (1929) and *El amor brujo* (1932), down to Ernesto Sabato's *Sobre héroes y tumbas* (1962) and Medina's *Striptease*.

The sexual frankness of *Monte* concerns forthrightly portrayed lesbianism, described in a first-person narrative by a small-town loser. The point-by-point details of her experiences are highlighted through an effective rhetorical strategy: she is the aggressive "masculine" partner. Her affairs are unconscious parodies of the tango-like love stories in which the prevailing perspective is that of the flinty-eyed and firm-jawed dominant macho who is heartlessly betrayed by the fickle daughters of Eve:

16. Buenos Aires: Ediciones de la Flor, 1976.
17. Buenos Aires: Ediciones de la Flor, 1976.
18. Roffé's first novel, *Llamado al puf* (1972), is included by Francine R. Masiello in her review essay "Contemporary Argentine Fiction: Liberal (Pre-)texts in a Reign of Terror." I find it difficult to be quite as severe as Masiello is in identifying "liberal" strategies for abiding by censorship in Argentina, particularly when so many have written and published at great personal sacrifice.

Con Paola vivimos un romance de película francesa, grandes eu-
forias y terribles incertidumbres, de acuerdo a su personalidad al-
tisonante y loca. En poco tiempo me enganchó totalmente. Luego
sus propósitos avanzaron mucho más, me exigió un compromismo
formal. Quería una fiesta y una alianza. Necesitaba el mayor de los
ridículos para satisfacer sus delirios. Yo, una veleta, le hice caso. Me
puse a trabajar como una burra para reunir dinero y cumplir con los
requisitos de un novio enamorado y respetuoso de las normas de la
sociedad. Para colmo, Paola había elegido una alianza de oro, de las
gruesas. Tuve que agarrar de punto a un pibe rengo que recién co-
menzaba a laburar con los bonos, arreglar una sociedad momen-
tánea con él y salir a vender, llevándolo de carnada. Creo que ya dije
que la gente siempre se ablanda con los desgraciados. De todos
modos, en poco tiempo, con el plazo que me había dado Paola, sólo
llegué a reunir la plata para uno de los anillos, el de la novia y unos
mangos más para el lunch. . . .
El día del compromiso fue apoteótico. Uno de los amigos maricas
de Paola nos había prestado la casa y la mersa en pleno se congregó
a festejar la realización de nuestro idilio. Pensar que no sentí vergüenza en ningún momento, por el contrario, estaba posesionada
de mi papel, el papel que representé auténticamente sin advertir
que era una burla grotesca de mi propia desgracia. Coloqué el anillo
en el dedo de Paola, casi temblando y la besé en los labios. Hubo
efusivos aplausos. Pero nuestro noviazgo oficial duró apenas una
semana.[19]

(Paola and I lived a French movie romance, grand euphorias and
terrible uncertainties, in accord with her high-flying and crazy personality. Before long she had me hooked completely. Then her de-
signs went even further: she demanded we be formally engaged.
She wanted a party and a wedding ring. She required the biggest
farce to satisfy her wild ideas. I, going along, respected her wishes.
I set to work like an animal to raise the money and to comply with
the demands on a loving fiancé who respects society's norms. Moreover, Paola had picked out a gold wedding ring, one of the thick
ones. I had to bring in a lame kid who'd just started working the
bond racket and put together a partnership with him on the spot to
get out there and sell, using him as bait. I think I already said that
people give in when unfortunates are involved. Anyway, within a
short time, and within the period of time Paola had given me, I was
only able to raise the money for one of the rings, the fiancée's, and a
few bucks for the lunch. . . .
The day of the engagement party was a huge success. One of

---

19. *Monte de Venus*, pp. 105–6, 107. Further citations will be made by page
number in the text.

Paola's queer friends lent us his place, and the whole goon platoon turned out to celebrate our idyll come true. Just think, I experience no sense of shame at any time. Quite the contrary, I was caught up in my role, a role that I played sincerely without catching on that it was a grotesque mockery of my own misfortune. Almost trembling, I placed the ring on Paola's finger, and I kissed her on the lips. There were effusive applauses. But our official engagement barely lasted a week.)

This account is a rehash of countless love stories, both trashy ones and more elevated literary ones. Were the narrator-protagonist a man, his tale would be a stereotyped repetition of hackneyed clichés, punctuated by drearily explicit couplings. As the story of a lesbian, however, the narrative takes on the freshness unavoidably associated with the first unveilings of a taboo shrouded in luridly suggestive mystery. It was hard enough for the guardians of Argentine morality to accept the virtual canonization of the rags-to-riches actress-concubine Evita Perón. And prostitutes have only been tolerated in literature if they come to a suitably horrible end.[20] But a novel that gives voice to an aggressive lesbian, one whose inverted behavior threatens sacred institutions by parodying them with notable fidelity, clearly represents a new threshold in the corruption of the national moral fiber.

The chapters describing Roffé's protagonist-lover's repeated subjections to Cupid's indiscriminate humiliations alternate with the story of another "typical" citizen, a young woman who resumes an interrupted secondary education by attending an evening adult program. These sections are ostensibly innocuous—at least they are free of the explicit sexuality that characterizes the first-person narration. Nevertheless, the women attending the night school do engage in random and basically heterosexual erotic discussions, often based on the physical quirks of their teachers. These sections are a loose-jointed series of vignettes, an Argentine version of Leo Rosten's *The Education of Hyman Kaplan* (albeit without any degree of ameliorating humor). The sketches concerning the grab-bag assortment of has-been students not much interested in serious educational pursuits are merciless in the way they zero in on circumstances that vitiate any pretense at learning. The teachers ap-

20. See in passing Domingo F. Casadevall, *El tema de la mala vida en el teatro nacional* (Buenos Aires: Guillermo Kraft, 1957).

pear to have been trained as insane-asylum wardens rather than as torchbearers of "Liberating Knowledge." The administrators are tin-badge tyrants—iron maidens whose sadism would be exquisite if they were not presented so ridiculously as poor copies of Argentine military figures:

> La Pechugona, firme como un sargento, se colocaba en la puerta del colegio a inspeccionar a las alumnas que entraban. Con la cabeza erguida, un tanto imperativa, el traste saliente y las piernas flacas, parecida a una gallina bataraza, la vice, con sus dobles pechugas listas a estallar en cualquier momento, humillaba a las chicas que tenían la cara demasiado pintada o las polleras muy cortas o algún escote por debajo de la clavícula. Les exigía que se quitaran la pintura facial o que arrojaran el chicle o las enviaba de vuelta a su casa, después de gritonearlas, ridiculizarlas o simplemente amonestarlas. Si no era monja, la que pasaba el filtro de la vice se dirigía a su curso y trataba de no dejarse ver más por la Pechugona, por si acaso se le había escapado algún detalle que reprochar. Algunas, más audaces, merodeaban por la sala de profesores con el objeto de saber cuál era la materia insalvable, concertar una cita, discutir una nota, curiosear un rato, perder el tiempo. Claro, que dispuestas a salir corriendo ni bien los enormes pechos de la vice echaran a perder sus enriedos. (p. 123)

(Busty, ramrod straight like a sergeant, would place herself at the door of the school in order to inspect the students who came in. With her head held high, a little imperatively, her protruding butt and her skinny legs, looking every bit like a speckled chicken, the Vice, her boobs ready to burst at any moment, would humiliate those girls whose faces were painted too much, or whose dresses were too short, or whose necklines were below their collarbones. She would make them remove their makeup or throw their gum out, or she would send them home after shouting at them, ridiculing them, or just simply admonishing them. Unless she was a nun, the girl who squeaked by would go off to class, hoping Busty wouldn't look at her again and find some little detail she might have missed to complain about. Some, the more audacious women, hung about the teachers' room with the object of finding out what subject was the toughest, making an appointment, to argue about a grade, to snoop around a bit, or to waste time. Of course, always ready to run off as soon as the Vice's enormous breasts arrived to spoil their intrigues.)

The teachers are pathetic in their incompetence: what they do know tends to be useless and often a cynical distortion of true intellectual inquiry. But no matter, since they are incapable of teaching anything anyway. One example will suffice: the civics professor is the author of books that enjoy official endorsement by the Ministry of Education because they are so opportunistically shallow as to support all official myths unquestioningly and to challenge none critically. By the same token, the educational facilities would be charmingly idiosyncratic if they were not so blatantly counterproductive of both teaching and learning. Thus, adult women are forced to use tables and chairs designed for what are euphemistically called "little people." The physical discomfort and concomitant decline in morale on the part of the initially eager students are presented with unwaveringly sardonic scrutiny by the narrator. The two threads of the novel come together in a dramatically effective surprise ending. Julia's story has been told as a sort of oral history to the literature professor, the only teacher who seems sympathetic to the students. Responding to claims that the latter is interested in first-hand "life experiences" for a novel she wishes to write, the hapless Julia is tricked into revealing not only her past transgressions but also her passions for the teacher. With the resulting tapes in hand, the teacher is able to demand successfully that Julia turn her illegitimate son over to the teacher. Julia thus provides the virgin priestess of knowledge, who is of course the lesbian protagonist of the other thread of the story, with a longed-for son to endow with the blessings of learning and human kindness that she purports to embody. The novel ends with Julia's panegyric, a virtual *planctus et lamenta in hac lacrymarum valle*:

> Me estafaron. Es la única palabra apropiada que se me ocurre para comenzar a ser yo, aunque parezca mentira, quien termine la historia. He dado miles de vueltas antes de prender este aparato y sentarme, ahora sola, aquí, en un cuarto de mi casa, a decir, simplemente, que estoy desesperada. Dios mío, cuántas cosas pueden pasar en unos meses, apenas, o en unas pocas horas, o con una sola palabra en una milésima de segundo. Pero antes que nada que quede claro que soy una persona con más bronca que tristeza. Mi bronca es lo único noble que tengo. No podría ser de otra manera que yo me pusiera a contar todo esto. Trato de ordenar mi pensamiento, no es fácil. Por momentos me asalta el desasosiego y unos deseos locos de romper el grabador. Sin embargo, continúo acá, creyendo que así podré desahogarme. (p. 267)

> (They cheated me. That's the only appropriate word that occurs to me that will allow me to be the one, as much of a lie as it might

appear, to finish this story. I have gone over and over it before turning this machine on and sitting down, now alone, here, in a room in
my house, to say, quite simply, that I am desperate. My God, how
many things can happen in one month, or in a few hours, or with a
single word in a thousandth of a second? But before anything else, I
would like to make it clear that I am more angry than I am sad. My
anger is the only noble thing left to me. I have no choice but to tell
all this. I try to order my thoughts, but it isn't easy. From one moment to the next anxiety assaults me, along with wild urges to
smash the tape recorder. But here I remain, believing that only in
this way can I ease my pain.)

The general context of complete institutional collapse in the
face of vain attempts by the self-appointed authorities and their
willing subalterns to shore up national myths is enhanced in
the novel by the "log" kept by the night-school student. This
log chronicles point-by-point the economic, cultural, and political chaos of the early seventies, the time in which the novel
is set. While *Monte* is not documentary fiction, these elements,
including Julia's oral history, contribute to the overall portrayal
of the crises of a specific society in the process of a time-bound
dissolution.

Both the female protagonists in Roffé's novel, the lesbian and
the night-school student, are in their respective (and eloquently
unconscious) fashions presented as exemplars of Miss Argentina. And both are ironic witnesses to a society suffering termi-
nal entropy. As such, they are far removed from the eponymic
heroine of *Amalia*, the Princess of Redemptive Good, who
struggled against the Satanic dictator Rosas in José Mármol's
historical novel concerning the social and political crises of the
young Argentine nation. Nor are they the victorious Amazons
some feminists would prefer to see projected by fictional accounts of the final liberation of woman from a macho-controlled
society. Silvina Bullrich's pathetic flowers of Argentine womanhood are more the accepted norm, as are the smoldering volcanoes of frustration in Clarice Lispector's Brazilian masterpieces. Both writers are recognized for their valuable images of
their experiences of women (usually upper middle class) in
their respective societies and in Latin America in general. Julia
and Barú are, rather, martyrs not just to the degradation of
women but also to the dismal failure of a whole society of
which they are sadly paradigmatic embodiments.

V

Of all of the Argentine writers born between 1930 and 1945, none has attracted greater international attention than Manuel Puig. If Medina is the author whose works have sold the most copies in Argentina, Puig (whose works have been mostly unavailable in Argentina for reasons of censorship) is the one who has been translated into English and who has been extensively studied among academics.[21] This does not mean that Puig is the best writer of his generation: questions of excellence are too relative and too unreliable to serve as the only criterion for analytical criticism. Puig—like many of the writers whose works are discussed in this study—has not yet produced a work with the resonance of, say, *Cien años de soledad*. One might say that *La traición de Rita Hayworth* (1968), his first novel, is still his best, but that is hardly a comforting comment for a novelist as widely praised as Puig.

One of the major features of Puig's novels is his enormous skill in assimilating diverse forms of so-called subliterature, giving his works their "readerly" as well as their more experimental "writerly" configuration. Indeed, his novels all involve intertextual relationships with cultural phenomena beyond the written word, and Puig is most known for his use of materials from the mass-media movie spectacle. This usage, as it was in *Traición*, is particularly evident in *El beso de la mujer araña* (1976).

On the level of a readerly and rather sensationalistic novel, *Beso* is the story of two prisoners: Molina, a homosexual incarcerated for seducing a minor, and Arregui, a political activist from whom the police are attempting to extract information concerning terrorist plans. The police have placed them in the same cell hoping that Molina, in exchange for his freedom, will be able to obtain from Arregui the information that torture has not been able to extract. Instead, the two become lovers (despite Arregui's clear heterosexuality), and they pass the time discussing a half-dozen popular movies whose plots Molina recounts at great length. When Molina is released, he attempts to contact Arregui's comrades and is killed by them when they realize that he is being tailed by the police, who suspected that contact would be arranged.

21. For a bibliographic listing of the extensive criticism on Puig, see Juan Armando Epple, "Bibliografía de Manuel Puig y sobre él." This section is an expanded version of my review of the novel in *Latin American Literary Review*, no. 14 (1979):73–74.

In general terms, there is a clear juxtaposition between the deep affection that develops between the two men in the isolated "idyllic" confinement of their cell and the shattering, impersonal attitudes of the outside world, embodied in the prison system and the plan to exploit Molina:

—No sé si me entendés. . . pero aquí estamos los dos solos, y nuestra relación, ¿cómo podría decirte?, la podemos moldear como queremos, nuestra relación no está presionada por nadie.
—Sí, te escucho.
—En cierto modo estamos perfectamente libres de actuar como queremos el uno respecto al otro, ¿me explico? Es como si estuviéramos en una isla desierta. Una isla en la que tal vez estemos solos años. Porque, sí, fuera de la celda están nuestros opresores, pero adentro no. Aquí nadie oprime a nadie. Lo único que hay, de perturbador, para mi mente. . . cansada, o condicionada o deformada. . . es que alguien me quiere tratar bien, sin pedir nada a cambio.
—Bueno, eso no sé. . .
—¿Cómo que no sabés?
—No me sé explicar.
—Vamos, Molina, no me salgas con ésas. Concentrate, y se te van a aclarar las ideas.
—Bueno, no pienses en nada raro, pero si yo te trato bien. . . es porque quiero ganarme tu amistad, y por qué no decirlo. . . tu cariño. Igual que trato bien a mi mamá porque es una persona buena que nunca hizo mal a nadie, porque la quiero, porque es buena, y quiero que ella me quiera. . . Y vos sos una persona muy buena, muy desinteresada, que se ha jugado la vida por un ideal muy noble. . . . Y no mires para otro lado, ¿te da vergüenza?
—Sí, un poco. . . . Pero te miro de frente, ¿yes?[22]

(—I don't know if you understand me . . . but here we are, all alone, and when it comes to our relationship, how should I put it? We could make any damn thing out of it we want; our relationship isn't pressured by anyone.
—Yes, I'm listening.
—In a sense we're perfectly free to behave however we choose with respect to one another, am I making myself clear? It's as if we were on some desert island. An island on which we may have to remain alone together for years. Because, well, outside of this cell we may have our oppressors, yes, but not inside. Here no one oppresses the other. The only thing that seems to disturb me . . . be-

22. *El beso de la mujer araña*, pp. 206–7. The translation that follows is taken from *Kiss of the Spider Woman*, trans. Thomas Colchi, pp. 202–3. Further citations will be made by page number in the text.

cause I'm exhausted, or conditioned or perverted . . . is that someone wants to be nice to me, without asking anything back for it.
—Well, about that I don't know . . .
—What do you mean you don't know?
—I can't explain it.
—Come on, Molina, don't try to pull that on me. Concentrate,
and you'll know what it is you're thinking, soon enough.
—Well, don't get the idea anything's strange, but if I'm nice to
you . . . it's because I want to win your friendship, and, why not say
it? . . . your affection. Same as I want to be good to my mom
because she's a nice person, who never did anybody any harm, because I love her, because she's nice, and I want her to love me . . .
And you too are a very nice person, very selfless, and you've risked
your life for a very noble ideal . . . And don't be looking the other
way, am I embarrassing you?
—Yes, a little . . . But I'm looking at you, see?

Thus, the image of a personal relationship that can transcend
an oppressive reality is juxtaposed with an even clearer image
of the destruction of such a relationship by a specific sociopolitical reality. To be sure, the entire novel is flagrantly hokey
in terms of plot: the placing together of a Molina and an Arregui would appear to contravene elementary principles of veri-
similitude, given the historical and political contexts involved.
Yet herein lies an important semiological aspect of the novel:
the "truth" resides not in any documentary accuracy—one can
seek such truth in the work of Amnesty International—but
rather in the meaningful elements that produce an independent meaning (that of the "false," overtly fictive novel) that is
homologous in some way with the patterns of meaning acceptable to the fiction's presumed reading public. In this sense, although the plot details of Puig's novel are highly fictive, the
structural patterns they give rise to possess a recognizable sociocultural meaning. Which leads us to the "writerly" aspects
of *Beso.*

Writerly novel is Roland Barthes's term for a work that, instead of providing a fully structured text, demands that the
reader establish a controlling pattern for apparently unstruc-
tured elements: each reader writes his own relatively definitive
text.[23] As such a novel, *Beso* involves at least five narrative levels

23. On "writerly" fiction, see the sections regarding contemporary concepts
of the novel in Jonathan Culler, *Structuralist Poetics: Structuralism, Linguistics,
and the Study of Literature.*

that are distinguished in part typographically. On an immediate narrative level that characterizes the novel as a whole (in the sense that it is the framework that embodies the rest of the novel), there are the dialogues between Molina and Arregui: details concerning their personal lives, the homosexual involvement of the former and the political commitment of the latter, the exchange of commentaries on the films that Molina describes. In conjunction with Molina's personal story, there appears a series of footnotes concerning psychological and sociological theories on homosexual behavior, ranging from Freud to Marcuse. These notes are interesting less for the scientific opinion they provide than for their emphasis on homosexuality as a constellation of behavior patterns that caricature and criticize bourgeois sex roles and marriage conventions (see, for example, the note on pp. 154–55).[24]

These notes have an important function as part of a pattern of reference to three aspects of sexuality: (1) the homosexual demimonde that Molina represents; (2) the syrupy and romanticized relations that are at the center of the plots of the awful 1940s movies that Molina recalls in such loving detail (unconsciously parodying his own unaccepted life-style by sympathizing with the impossibly sentimental man-woman relationships of those movies); and (3) the impersonal and clinically detached commentaries contained in the footnotes. It is in the shifting patterns among these three elements that we may best see *Beso* function, not as a documentary novel concerned with the texture of sociopolitical issues as lived by a series of "psychologically whole" characters, but as an example of the contemporary novel's concern for the gain derived from juxtaposing in different structural patterns an inventory of potentially meaningful elements.[25]

In addition to the immediate narrative and the footnotes, on a third level we have Molina's detailed plot summaries of films; Arregui is the "public" for Molina's secondary, derived narratives. There is, of course, a process of narrative reduplication

24. The use of footnotes as an ingredient of fiction is examined by Shari Benstock, "At the Margin of Discourse: Footnotes in the Fictional Text."
25. Robert Scholes sees much contemporary fiction as "structural fabulation"—that is, writing that is purportedly fictive but actually more interested in semiological patterns than in the character psychology associated with earlier fiction. Although his *Structural Fabulation: An Essay on Fiction of the Future* focuses on science fiction (hence a pun on the acronym "SF"), it is because Scholes sees such fiction as paradigmatic of structural fabulation.

operant here: Puig's novel is an account of Molina's account of the love stories presented by a certain type of film. It is from the interplay among these separate discourses that the novel's eloquent irony derives: Puig's novel is to be taken seriously; the films are to be taken as so much sentimental Hollywood drivel by the readers of the novel because of the extensive differences in register between the two. Finally, Molina's accounts are to be understood as unconsciously pathetic to the extent that they parody the latter and make a point concerning the former—stressing Molina's sociocultural dependency, despite his socioculturally defined deviancy.

All of the films recounted by Molina involve concepts of romantic love, idealized man-woman relationships, and unconsciously exploitive affection and emotion. They are American, Mexican, and German productions (the latter a Nazi propaganda film shown in Argentina during the first Peronista period). Molina's extensive verbal re-creation of these films fills the novel. However, from a writerly point of view, these re-creations are not simple diversions, easy as they may be to read. Instead, they demonstrate Puig's demythificational belief—a belief that has underlain all his fiction—that the examination of the mass, popular culture of a people can, when presented as a meaningful component of the text and not just its unintegrated surface gloss, provide a significant portrait of the system of values of that people.

In this regard, Molina's understanding of foreign films is just as ironically revealing as is his identification with a strictly Argentine popular culture. Molina's relationship to the films, his identification with the characters, and the exchanges between him and Arregui all constitute a significant and productive pattern of derived meanings (that is, of meanings derived by implication through strategic juxtapositions and not merely from what is said). From these derived meanings there emerges a trenchantly demythificational portrait of traditional man-woman stereotypes and their integral place in a repressive society:

> —¿Qué querés [Molina] que te cuente de ella?
> —Lo que quieras, el tipo de chica que es.
> —Tiene veinticuatro años, Molina. Dos menos que yo.
> —Trece menos que yo.
> —Siempre fue revolucionaria. Primero le dio por. . . bueno, con vos no voy a tener escrúpulos. . . le dio por la revolución sexual.

—Contame por favor.

—Ella es de un hogar burgués, gente no muy rica, pero vos sabés, desahogada, casa de dos pisos en Caballito. Pero toda su niñez y juventud se pudrió de ver a los padres destruirse uno al otro. Con el padre que engañaba a la madre, pero vos sabés lo que quiero decir.

—No, ¿qué querés decir?

—La engañaba al no decirle que necesitaba de otras relaciones. Y la madre se dedicó a criticarlo delante de la hija, se dedicó a ser víctima. Yo no creo en el matrimonio, en la monogamía más precisamente.

—Pero qué lindo cuando una pareja se quiere toda la vida.

—¿A vos te gustaría eso?

—Es mi sueño.

—¿Y por qué te gustan los hombres entonces?

—Qué tiene que ver. . . Yo quisiera casarme con un hombre para toda la vida.

—¿Sos un señor burgués en el fondo, entonces?

—Una señora burguesa.

—¿Pero no te das cuenta que todo es un engaño? Si fueras mujer no querrías eso.

—Y como eso es imposible, porque si él es hombre querrá a una mujer, bueno, nunca te vas a poder desengañar.

—Seguí con lo de tu compañera, no tengo ganas de hablar de mí. (pp. 49–50)

(—What do you [Molina] want me to tell you about her?

—Whatever you want to say, what kind of girl she is.

—She's twenty-four, Molina. Two years younger than me.

—Thirteen less than me.

—She always was a revolutionary. At first in terms of . . . well, I won't hesitate with you . . . in terms of the sexual revolution.

—Please, tell me about it.

—She comes from a bourgeois family, people who aren't very rich, but, you know, comfortable enough, two-story house in Caballito. But she spent her whole childhood and adolescence tormented by watching her parents destroying one another. With a father who deceived the mother, but you know what I mean . . .

—No, what?

—Deceived her by not telling her how he needed outside relationships. And the mother devoted herself to criticizing him in front of the daughter, devoted herself to being the martyr. I don't believe in marriage—or in monogamy, to be more precise.

—But how marvelous when a couple loves each other for a lifetime.

—You'd really go for that?

—It's my dream.
—So why do you like men then?
—What's that got to do with it? . . . I'd like to marry a man for the rest of my life.
—So you're a regular bourgeois gentleman at heart, eh, Molina?
—Bourgeois lady, thank you.
—But don't you see how all that's nothing but a deception? If you were a woman, you wouldn't want that.
—I'm in love with a wonderful guy and all I ask is to live by his side for the rest of my life.
—And since that's impossible, because if he's a guy he wants a woman, well, you're never going to undeceive yourself.
—Go on about your girl, I don't feel like talking about me.)
(pp. 43–44)

It is within the context of this dialectic criticism that Arregui abandons his own bourgeois and revolutionary inhibitions and "gives" himself sexually to Molina. Thus, the extensive film plot summaries are not meant to be read as such. They must be decoded within the controlling sociopolitical context of the (verisimilarly implausible) imprisonment of the two men and the relationship that develops between them and changes each one's preconceived ideas concerning personal freedoms.

On an additional narrative level we have Molina's conversations concerning his "cooperation" with the prison director (he agrees to cooperate but does not, hence his death at the end of the novel; Arregui we may safely presume is condemned to die under further torture) and the police report on the surveillance of Molina after his release from prison. The former excludes Arregui and implicitly comments on the system of exploitation that conflicts with the relationship between the two men. The latter excludes Molina as well and underscores his loss of control over a situation that he helped to manipulate in favor of that relationship.

The all-engulfing waves of anonymous oppression close over the tenuous and ultimately impossible idyll that two sensitive human beings have attempted to establish in place of an unmanipulatable reality. And however manipulatable of reality fiction may be, the complex patterns Puig sets up against that reality must in the end yield to its oppressive presence; thus the abolition of Molina and Arregui as the internal fabulators of the novel. In this sense, the love between them may sound as romantically sentimental as one of the former's favorite films.

Nevertheless, the context in which the love manifests itself and the perspectives on both general Western society and Argentine sociopolitics make *Beso* a complex example of narrative demythification.[26]

VI

Puig's novel is only one of a series of Argentine titles that focus on the guerrilla phenomenon in the sixties and early seventies in order to demythify Argentina through its megapolitan and megalomanic Buenos Aires. In addition to Puig's *El beso de la mujer araña*, perhaps the best example of this genre is Ernesto Sabato's *Abbadón el exterminador*.[27] Although Julio Cortázar's *El libro de Manuel* (1973) is set in Paris, an Argentine guerrilla group concerned with Argentine problems is involved, and Marta Lynch's *La penúltima versión de la Colorada Villanueva* (1978) is, in a sense, the culmination of such narratives, set in a time when Argentina is at "peace" and the guerrillas have been liquidated.[28]

With Jorge Asís's *Los reventados* we have a totally different focus on the same pattern of events.[29] The perspective of the novel is specifically Peronista, chronicling Perón's short-lived triumphant return to Buenos Aires in 1973, almost twenty years after his rout by the Revolución Libertadora in 1955. (Perón lived just long enough after his return to be reelected president; he was succeeded by his incompetent wife, María Isabel. She managed to stay in power until the military once again assumed power in 1976: Latin America's first woman president did not, unfortunately, leave a glorious legacy.)

Los reventados, like Medina's novel, is aggressively colloquial:

26. Note should also be taken of Abelardo Arias's novel *De tales cuales* (Buenos Aires: Editorial Sudamericana, 1973), which deals with a pair of hippie homosexual revolutionaries. See my review in *Books Abroad* 48 (1974):541.

27. Buenos Aires: Editorial Sudamericana, 1974. See my review in *Revista iberoamericana*, no. 90 (1975):148–50, and the controversial opinions published in *Crisis*, no. 16 (1974):49–53.

28. David Viñas, the most important of the novelists of the Generación del 55, has published his own version of recent Argentine political events and their tragic effect on individual human rights: *Cuerpo a cuerpo* (Mexico City: Siglo XXI, 1979).

29. All quotations are from the Buenos Aires: Editorial Sudamericana, 1977, edition and will be cited by page number in the text. Andrés Avellaneda provides a less-than-indulgent critique of the best-seller aspects of Asís in "'Best-seller' y código represivo en la narrativa argentina del ochenta: el caso Asís."

the title means "blown apart" or "exploded" (as in the case of an object) or "squeezed dry" (as in the case of an exhausted person); it also has the connotation of violent sexual penetration. The novel is a sort of calendar of the new Peronista period inaugurated by Perón's return to Buenos Aires in June 1973 after Héctor Cámpora, his party's puppet candidate, has assumed the presidency. Three segments focus on three crucial moments. (1) A prologue and epilogue are set on 25 September 1973, exactly four months after Cámpora was sworn in. On this day, the right-wing Peronista labor-leader José Rucci was assassinated in the growing urban guerrilla warfare and disorder that graphically highlighted the unchecked decline into chaos and the inevitable military coup of 1976. (2) A twelve-chapter narrative centers on Perón's return on 20 June, a return marked by severe violence that anticipated the radical disorder of the new Peronista period. This narrative, an "exemplum" of the general tenor of events established by the prologue and summarized by the epilogue, concerns the abortive attempt by a ragtag group of go-getters—true citizens of the Peronista constituency—to exploit the leader's return by hawking slipshod posters and pamphlets along the route from Ezeiza airport to Buenos Aires. (3) A series of intercalated vignettes frames the chapters of the exemplary novel. These vignettes are sketches of the *reventados* as they make plans between the 25 May inauguration and the 20 June return of Perón. The protagonists of the commercial venture are all experts at *pedaleando*, at *bicicleteando*, at *haciendo rosquete*, phrases that metonymically describe the street-savvy hustling of the seedy man-on-the-make in and around the haunts of Calle Corrientes and the Tribunales halls of justice:

> Dibujó su idea Cristóbal.
> —Doblado, ves, como si fuera un folleto. En la tapa le encajamos la transparencia, fijate, la jeta de Perón, todo un kilo. Al abrirse, del lado de adentro le metemos, yo qué sé, palabras de Perón, frases, hay montones, o las veinte verdades del peronismo.
> —Claro—entendió Willy—, podemos hacer como si fuera un diploma, o una carta de Perón a su pueblo.
> —Eso mismo, como una carta de agradecimiento al pueblo, por haberlo ido a esperar a Ezeiza. Y le encajamos la firma de Perón abajo—dijo Cristóbal—, sacamos la firma de cualquier solicitada.
> La idea era magnífica, pensó Willy, pero también, como toda idea, perfeccionable, porque se le ocurrió meterle algo en la parte de

atrás, la contratapa, viste. Repentinamente Cristóbal propuso meter una foto de la Eva, hay tantas, pero se arrepintió de inmediato porque había que mandar hacer otro fotocromo, y eran más gastos; además Willy dijo que estaban publicadísimas las fotos de la Eva.
—Para ser novedá, tenés que conseguir por lo menos una foto de la Eva desnuda—Willy.
Rieron un poco, les hacía bien. Cuando detuvieron la risa, fue Willy quien enunció la justa.
Listo, le encajamos los dedos de la victoria, en *Ve*, y le hacemos dibujado el escudo justicialista. (pp. 45–46)

(Cristóbal outlined his idea. "Fold over, see, like a pamphlet. On the cover we put one of the transparencies, see, of Perón's mug, all real fancy. When you open it, on the inside we can put, let's see, some of Perón's words, there are so many, of the Twenty Truths of Peronism."

"Sure," Willy caught on, "we can make it look like a diploma, or a letter from Perón to the people."

"That's it, something like a letter of gratitude to the people for having gone to Ezeiza [International Airport] to welcome him. And we can put Perón's signature at the bottom," Cristóbal said, "we can get the signature from some document."

The idea was magnificent, Willy thought, but also, like any idea, unprovable. Because he had the idea to put something on the back, get it. Cristóbal quickly suggested using a picture of Eva, there are so many, but he regretted it immediately because it would mean ordering another color cut, and that would mean more expense. Besides, Willy said that photos of Eva were everywhere.

"In order for it to be something new, you'd have to at least get one of Eva in the nude," Willy said.

This made them laugh a little, and it did them good. When their laughter subsided, it was Willy who put his finger on it.

That's it, we'll put his fingers raised in victory, the V sign, and we can do a sketch of the Justicialist shield.)

Asís's use of these socially marginal individuals to chronicle a key moment in the new Peronista period is noteworthy. There are successful contemporary examples of Lukácsian historical novels in which the protagonists are the main figures in the historical events: Robert Coover's *The Public Burning*, Alejo Carpentier's *El recurso del método*, Gabriel García Márquez's *El otoño del patriarca*, Augusto Roa Bastos's *Yo el Supremo*. But Asís's novel fulfills the Rosenkrantz and Guildenstern imperative: the perspective is in terms of those affected, in expanding waves of impact, by an event rather than in terms of its principal agents, who often are oblivious or unconcerned as regards the shock effects they create.

Needless to say, Asís's strategy is much more effective in accomplishing a demythification, for it shows the interplay between illusion and reality without needing to highlight the latter or portray directly the agents of the destruction of the former: [30]

Poster poster a los maravillosos poster de nuestro maravilloso General; Willy veía que Rocamora había abandonado su puesto en la banquina y venía caminando hacia él, lentamente, ya se le estaba acercando. No le preguntó qué quería porque se le arrimó una viejita para preguntarle cuánto valía la foto.

—Quinientos pesos, abuela—respondió Willy.

—Qué ladrones—dijo la viejita; Willy sonrió

—Se me enojó la abuelita—dijo Willy, simpático.

La abuelita siguió su camino, maldiciendo a los ladrones, envuelta en una bandera argentina.

Poster poster poster a los magníficos poster del General; se le había arrimado Rocamora.

—Dicen que vienen unos con banderas verdes. Son de la Juventud Sindical Peronista, los de Rucci, viste. ¿Sentís?—preguntó Rocamora—, oí el quilombo que hacen.

Poster poster poster de nuestro idolatrado General y estaban aproximándose alrededor de setenta tipos con banderas verdes, y cada tipo traía un bombo, por eso hacían tanto barullo, si hasta parecían más.

Poster poster de nuestro heroico General y todavía Willy no había vendido un solo poster y claro, si todavía no había comenzado a caer el grueso, Cristóbal, fijate, la gente que caminaba era suelta, no ves, muchas familias, chicos, matrimonios, alguno hasta con un perrito; continuamente pasaba gente desfilando y Willy ofrecía, con mucha cancha poster poster del General, pero la gente lo pasaba de largo. Como alambre caído, pensaba Rocamora. (pp. 53–54)

(Poster poster get your marvelous posters of our marvelous General: Willy saw how Rocamora had left his place on the curb and was walking toward him, now he was getting close to him. He didn't ask him what he wanted because a little old lady came up to him to ask him how much the photograph cost.

"Five hundred pesos, grandma," Willy answered.

"What thieves," the old lady said. Willy smiled.

"Grandma got mad at me," Willy, always charming, said.

30. On the direct portrayal of the Peróns in fiction, see Ernesto Goldar, *El peronismo en la literatura argentina*, and the dissertation by Andrés Avellaneda, "El tema del peronismo en la narrativa argentina."

The grandmother went on her way, cursing the thieves, wrapped up in an Argentine flag.
Poster poster poster get your magnificent posters of the General.
Rocamora had joined him.
"They say that some others are coming with green flags. They belong to the Peronist Youth Union, Rucci's group, see. Do you hear them," Rocamora asked, "listen to the racket they're making."
Poster poster poster of our idolized General and about seventy persons were coming up carrying green flags. Each person carried a drum, which is why they were making so much noise. It seemed like there were even more of them than there were.
Poster poster of our heroic General and Willy still hadn't sold a single poster and of course the bulk of people hadn't come along yet, Cristóbal, see, the people walking along were all strung out, don't you see, a lot of families, kids, couples, someone even leading a dog. People continued filing by and Willy, always clever, tried to hawk to them posters of the General. But the people went on by. Just like a downed line, Rocamora thought.)

In the vignettes that constitute the third component of the novel, Asís demonstrates Roberto Arlt's fabled ability to zero in on the gray and seedy humanscape that teems with all imaginable sorts of "life experiences" in the streets of downtown Buenos Aires.[31] As in Arlt's *Aguafuertes porteñas*, there is no attempt at psychological introspection. Indeed, the individuals involved are barely able to contemplate themselves or each other with significant comprehension. The emphasis is on grotesque traits that underline the moral, ethical, and sociopolitical bankruptcy of some very—and truly painfully—weak human beings caught in the tight web of society and an economic system that offers them no way out, no hope of success, honorable or otherwise. The only options for the *reventado* are suicide or to continue the frenetic attempts at street-hustling in the never-ending but equally never-fulfilling mazes of deals, angles, and hot tips.

The juxtaposition between these Arltian vignettes and the central narrative provides two self-sustaining levels of demythification in the novel. The vignettes are independent and mordant commentaries that serve to demythify the so-often romanticized Porteño man-in-the-street. For their impact, these sketches depend on the fact that the implied reader differs dia-

---

31. Asís has also continued Arlt's *Aguafuertes porteñas* with his own *Cuaderno de Oberdán Rocamora* (Buenos Aires: Rodolfo Alonso, 1977).

metrically from the individuals portrayed, beginning with a re-pudiation of both Peronismo and the self-serving commercial exploitation by the *reventados* of Perón's return. Even if an actual reader does not so differ, Peronismo is presented in such un-flattering terms—as in the very title of the novel—that he will perforce feel superior. The implied reader, as a reader of se-rious literature, is self-analytical, has the ability to compare the text of the vignettes intertextually with Arlt's and others' writ-ings, and is willing to accept the social bankruptcy of contem-porary Argentine society that the Peronista period serves to highlight.

On the other hand, the narrative of the commercial venture is demythifying in its overt juxtaposition of the glorious event with its complete debacle, as the disaster of the Gran Retorno is correlated with the collapse of the *reventados'* get-rich-quick scheme.[32] This correlation is overt and unmistakable because the progression of the commercial downfall of the *reventados* is interwoven in the narrative with a variety of devices (rumors among the crowd being particularly effective) that detail the failure of the spectacle organized around Perón's arrival (see, for example, p. 155).

Semantically, two intersecting levels in the novel correlate a political axis with a sociocultural one. On the first level, there is the maddeningly complex network of sociopolitical and ideo-logical relations involved in the Peronista movement of the mid-seventies. For many, Peronismo alternately made sense as an attempt at a renovating synthesis of a chaotic Argentine scene and refused to yield meaning because it was the essence of chaos. On a more general and less chronological level, there is the equally complex fabric of a metropolitan monster that feeds on many of the sociopolitical problems epitomized by the Per-onista experience. It is a monster that lives by an unwritten code (a meaningful if corrupt semiological infrastructure) that controls the interrelated realms (in a capitalist society) of eco-nomic and interpersonal relationships. For there is no doubt that in this setting the economic and the personal cannot be

---

32. Because of the violence, Perón landed at the Morón military airstrip rather than at Ezeiza. The thousands who thronged to see him along the high-way into Buenos Aires were, as a harbinger of things to come, disappointed and felt themselves deceived. When Perón appeared on television that evening, he was clearly a sick old man.

separated: one's contact with other human beings is a function of his participation in rigid, corrupting systems in which to be *sanito* ("clean," "ok") is to be an innocent and utter fool, at least as far as material survival is concerned.

Asís's novel, originally published in 1974 by the important journal *Crisis* (1973–1976), makes it clear that in the degraded jungle of Buenos Aires there is no hierarchy: *reventar* is a reflexive verb that describes an all-encompassing system: "Como Tarzán, agarrado de la liana, matando en la selva para que no me maten" (Like Tarzan, hanging from a liana, killing in the jungle to keep myself from getting killed; p. 203).

VII

Héctor Lastra's only novel, *La boca de la ballena*, belongs to a series of novels written since the fifties in which an immediately personal story is correlated in some way with the Peronista experience.[33] No matter what any given individual's position was, Perón affected the entire populace as profoundly as Hitler affected Germany. Ernesto Sabato's *Sobre héroes y tumbas* is perhaps the best work in this vein, establishing a network of relations between present and past events in the history of Argentina.[34] In the case of Lastra's novel, the specific point of reference is the final death throes of the Peronista government in 1955. It is a period of acute social and political disintegration, which Lastra's novel sets out to portray in terms of the decaying fabric of an oligarchic family. The family awaits the fall of Perón and the imposition of a military government with a religious enthusiasm reserved customarily for the promised triumph of the Messiah over the anti-Christ.

Ostensibly *Boca* is a first-person *Bildungsroman*. The young narrator proposes to write, from the perspective of young manhood, a record of his growing perception, during the early fifties when he was a child, of the world around him. He perceives his own family as a microcosm of that world and of a certain social class with a defined and restrictive set of values and

---

33. See the review by Stephen T. Clinton, *Books Abroad* 49 (1975):86. Citations from this novel will be by page number in the text.
34. Concerning the structural relationships of the characters in *Sobre héroes y tumbas*, see the chapter on Sabato in David William Foster, *Currents in the Contemporary Argentine Novel*.

opinions concerning the world outside the suffocating confines
of the family's fortressed compound. The individuals of this
outside world bring disruption to the values, activities, and
perspectives of the narrator's family. Moreover, it was through
contacts with these individuals that the narrator discovered the
flotsam and jetsam of humanity that took up residency during
the Peronista period in the shantytowns along the banks of the
Río de la Plata, at the literal and figurative foot of the stately
mansions that line the bluffs overlooking the floodplain of the
river. These huts were a typical sign of the Peronista policies. Their
inhabitants were provincials, the *cabecitas negras* who flocked to
the capital with the promise of good jobs, wages, and housing.
At the end of the Peronista period, although numerous low-
cost housing developments had been completed, the shanties
were still teeming. The military government was quick to tear
them down in a graphic gesture of demolishing the outward
signs of the Peronista society. At the end of the novel, the narrator returns to the shantytown after joining his family in the
joyous Te Deum celebrations upon the fall of Perón. He returns
seeking the friend that he has made there and the latter's family; he finds them and the town gone. In the bargain he is apparently raped by a vagrant who, as a last defense of the lost
legions, exacts a symbolic vengeance on the pitiful poor little
rich boy:

> Miré hacia las barrancas y no vi sus luces de festejo; vi las morta-
> jas de la infancia, el pálido desfilar de las telarañas, la imagen de mi
> abuelo, su estela de veneno y esa miserable condena a salas y ante-
> salas, a pasillos y estucos, a terrazas solitarias azotadas por la iner-
> cia y el hastío, esperándome. Vi el agua descompuesta del sótano,
> la vi ascender espesísima, ganar los escalones y arrasar las alfombras
> con sus grumos verdinegros. Vi mi cuarto, mi cama contra la pared
> tupida de hongos, mi cama de bronce y loza, mi despertar bajo los
> angelotes del techo, bajo sus ojos vacíos, y tuve miedo. Un miedo
> grave, más que doloroso, muy distinto de los demás miedos de mi
> vida. Un miedo gélido, visceral, que ni siquiera volvía a exhibirme el
> descampado, la estepa del desastre, porque esa estepa ya estaba en
> mí con todos sus lomos de ceniza, con todas sus chapas retorcidas y
> sus cadáveres de alambre. No obstante, de nuevo sin mirar lo que
> pisaba, de nuevo sin sentir los labios y las manos, sin sentir en las
> mejillas brisa alguna, traté de postergar el adiós definitivo y de re-
> conocer en medio del humo y de la oscuridad algo de los días del

pasado. Sí, traté de hallar aunque fuera una sombra, un destello, cualquier cosa a que aferrarme, cualquier cosa que no fuese aquella blandura informe bajo mis pies, aquel hedor malsano coagulándose en la niebla.[35]

(I looked toward the ravines, and I could not see their party lights. I saw the shrouds of childhood, the pale filing by of spider webs, the image of my grandfather, his wake of poison and that terrible sentence of salons and waiting rooms, of hallways and plaster, of solitary terraces lashed by inertia and boredom, waiting for me. I saw the decomposed water of the basement, I saw it rise thickly, reach the stairs and wash over the rugs with its green-black sludge. I saw my room, my bed against the wall thickly covered by mold, my brass and porcelain bed, my waking up under the angels painted on the ceiling, beneath their vacant eyes, and I was afraid. It was a deep fear, something other than painful, different from the other fears of my life. An icy, visceral fear, one that didn't even serve again to reveal to me the barren field, the steppe of disaster, because that steppe was within me with all of its ashen rises, with all of its twisted plates and its wire bodies. Nevertheless, once again not noticing what I stepped on, once again not feeling either my lips or my hands, without feeling any breeze on my cheeks, I tried to put off the final goodbye and to recognize amid the smoke and the darkness something of the bygone days. Yes, I tried to find at least a shadow, a trace, anything to hold on to, anything but that formless softness beneath my feet, that unhealthy stink clotting in the fog.)

The polarities of the novel are quick to emerge. It is important to note that Lastra's novel cuts in both directions. On the one hand, there is little sympathy for the Peronista ideal. The sorry lot of the shantytown dwellers is the most graphic indication of the need to demythify the demagoguery of the movement. On the other hand, the novel's handling of the metonymic features of the Gothic world of the oligarchy that supported the Revolución Libertadora of 1955 is unrestrainedly grotesque. One of the high points of the novel is the story of the family's sometime patriarch (the narrator's profligate maternal uncle who comes and goes) and his "courtesan," an aging and once highly placed cleric. Unlike so many novels concerning the Peronista decline and the subsequent iron-fisted military regency, Lastra's novel does not marshal a binary opposition between

---

35. *La Boca de la ballena*, p. 266. Further citations will be made by page number in the text.

the Good (us) and the Bad (them), with the ideological poles being determined by the author's stance toward Peronismo.[36] Some of the key signs in *Boca* are mansion versus shantytown, oligarchic narrator versus proletarian friend, youth versus maturity, family versus the world at large, heterosexuality versus homosexuality, reactionary religion versus proletarian politics. But these oppositions are not embodied in the narrative in terms of a fixed binary opposition that could loosely be summarized as Good versus Bad. Although two semantic realms are defined (in ideological terms, the oligarchy versus the Peronistas), in the final analysis they do not emerge as mutually exclusive opposites, but as variants of one uniform reality that has undergone a process of degradation.

The semiological axis of differentiation is provided by the privileged first-person narrator, who as the source of the text determines the quality of the signs he calls up. Rather than mediating between the Good and the Bad and identifying with the former, Lastra's narrator homologizes the superficially opposing signs so that the ultimate opposition is between him, as the violated offspring of a totally corrupt society, and all the signs of that society he has presented throughout the novel. Demythification in *Boca* is consequently the result of this process of homology and the subsequent I/it differentiation that so vividly concludes the novel. In a metaphoric sense, this is what the epigraph of the novel announces as its guiding structural principle:

> *Dicen ciertas crónicas, que la boca de la ballena tiene dientes gigantescos y tupidos como la estopa. Allí quedan apresados los peces chicos y también los grandes, junto a muchas inmundicias y resacas del mar, formando así una masa informe y putrefacta.*
>
> *Dicen otras crónicas, que los marineros de la Martinica—navegantes vigorosos del "Atlantic"—, caían desvanecidos en cubierta, por los hedores nauseabundos que despedían las bocas de las ballenas.* (p. 7)
>
> (*Certain chronicles say that the mouth of the whale has gigantic teeth, as tight as oakum. Small as well as large fish are caught in them, along with all sorts of flotsam and jetsam of the sea, creating a formless and putrid mass.*
>
> *Other chronicles say that the sailors of Martinique, vigorous navigators*

---

36. One of the best examples is Rodolfo Walsh's *Operación masacre* (1957), where the Bad is the Revolución Libertadora. See my comments on this text in Chapter 1 of this study.

of the Atlantic, would drop on the deck in a faint as a result of the nauseating stench that emanated from the mouths of the whales.)

VIII

The late seventies was not a halcyon time for young writers in Argentina: over a decade of iron-fisted rule by unvisionary military governments and of suicidal guerrilla activity within the context of a pretense at democracy had left the country exhausted, and cultural activities had been damaged seriously. Ediciones Corregidor was one of the few publishers in the seventies willing to present a young writer.

Hugo Corra's *Frontera sin retorno* (1978) is an excellent example of open, "writerly" fiction in recent Argentine literature, in contrast with the facile literature and translations of best-sellers being published in the hopes of gaining economic success. *Frontera* is writerly in the sense that it is framed as a meta-novel: it describes the activity of reading a novel and of undertaking the various interpretational and contextualizing tasks associated with the act of reading and of constructing (from the perspective of the reader) a phenomenological meaning. Specifically, Corra uses the hoary gambit of a retrieved manuscript—in this case the diary left by the long-since runaway father of the narrator's former *compañera*. Significantly, the diary's text is delayed, put off, despite the promises of the "prologue" and the repeated affirmations of the narrator that his goal is to publish the text. Thus, in the opening segments of *Frontera*, the diary is the missing center: perhaps the novel would have been more intriguing if Corra, like Macedonio Fernández in *Museo de la novela de la Eterna* (written in the twenties, but only published in 1967), had never included the much vaunted but eventually forthcoming text.

The crucial text, the missing man's diary, provides the narrator with a quest, and the narrative records his attempts to annotate the diary by providing information concerning the principal individuals involved, their interrelationships with the diary's compiler, along with his own alternatingly subjective and objective interpretations of these elements. The novel develops in terms of the shifting structural relations between these elements and the segments of the diary, which is in due course reproduced. Through this process, the narrator reveals fluctuating patterns and, most important, his own personal involvement with what he is investigating and interpreting: his text is semiologically unstable, and his reading of it postulates a series of converging and contradictory meanings. Central to all this is his realization that the narrator of the diary also describes a quest for a missing meaning and a "missing" narrator. Thus, the basic complexity of the novel derives from the homology developed among the novel, the annotations provided by the narrator (which constitute a secondary text with the various intercalated narratives), and the controlling text—the diary, which in turn opens up its own Pandora's box of texts and narratives.

The text of the diary could not stand alone and derives its novelistic importance from the structural embedding described above. Read by itself, it is a collection of short texts, most of them sketches. These texts echo a long line of writings concerning the drabness and flatness of life in our contemporary unheroic world and in the spiritually oppressive society of modern bourgeois Argentina, where irreflectiveness is a virtue and self-searching is considered an unproductive waste of time:

Eso sí: sé muy bien que, igual que hoy, me van a encontrar en el extremo perfecto y normalizador, donde caducan mis libertades individuales, esas libertades que aprendí a empujones y sopapos sin poder ejercerlas, sin ningún tipo de indulgencia con los demás ni conmigo mismo. La verdad es que estoy cansado. Sólo obedezco a la dictadura de las personas que me acompañan y quiero ser honesto de una vez, demostrarme que puedo conocerme. La intimidad es casi casi un misterio arqueológico escondido a miles de metros de mí mismo y tardaré bastante en alcanzarla. Sin embargo Raúl, el hombre que fui deja su identikit cotidiano, y se descubre tal cual es con la gente que tiene relación con su pasado, para dejar de sentirse solo. Porque los solos como yo trabajamos en los prostíbulos. . . . Es que Buenos Aires desdibuja a los hombres, los hace escalar y los mata de infarto, los construye y los desmorona, les da vida y los mata. Pero te digo que no es exactamente Buenos Aires. Me refiero a unos pocos, a los tristes cabecillas de esta gavilla de insensatos. Han capturado a Buenos Aires, lo tienen drogado en una pieza y lo recargan todos los días para paralizarlo. Todos están encantados con sus sendas peatonales pintadas de blanco, sus policías femeninas, sus homilías pastorales y el Trust Joyero Relojero, que tiene mucho que ver en todo esto. ¡Qué insignificante me siento! Por ese motivo necesito encontrar a Colores. Pero hasta que no llegue ese momento seguiré refugiado en mi embajada personal mientras mi familia patrulla con la hipocresía, esperando que salga para tratar de neutralizarme.[37]

(Just that: I know full well that, the same as today, they will find me at the perfect and normalizing extreme, where my individual liberties decline, those liberties that I learned by being shoved around and slapped without being able to exercise them, without any kind of indulgence toward others or toward myself. The truth is that I am tired. I only obey the dictatorship of those persons who accompany me, and I wish to be honest with myself, to show myself that I can know myself. Intimacy is really almost an archaeological mystery hidden thousands of meters from me, and I will take quite a long time to find it. Nevertheless, Raúl, the man I was, sets his daily identikit aside, to discover himself as he is with those who are related to his past, only to feel himself alone. Because the lonely like me work in brothels. . . . It's just that Buenos Aires frazzles people, it makes them scale high and it kills them with a heart attack, it builds them up and it makes them cave in, it gives them life and it kills them. But I say to you that it isn't exactly Buenos Aires. I am referring to a few, to the sad leaders of this pack of loons. They have captured Buenos Aires, they're holding him drugged in a room, and they give him a new jolt each day in order to paralyze him. Everybody is thrilled with the city's crosswalks painted white, its policewomen, its pastoral homilies and the Trust Jewelry and Watch Store, which has a lot to do in all this. How insignificant I feel! That's why I need to find Colores. But until that moment comes, I will remain secure in my personal embassy while my family is on patrol with its hypocrisy, waiting for me to come out so they can neutralize me.)

The narrator of the diary provides these texts and the controlling motif of the quest for the perhaps impossible fulfillment of a meaningful human existence in modern Buenos Aires. But it is the hierarchical structure of embedded narrator/quester that gives *Frontera* its particular texture as a novelistic document concerning the crushing frustration of visionary individuals in oppressive societies and of writers who would deal with them.

IX

The authors described in this chapter in no way constitute a movement or a group. Nor do they necessarily constitute a

37. *Frontera sin retorno*, pp. 55–56.

who's who of Argentine fiction in the seventies.[38] Like their U.S. counterparts, they may best be viewed as "disruptionists," as writers who take seriously the need to revolutionize literary forms, the ways for dealing discursively with sociopolitical realities, and the strategies for giving meaning to that reality through the semiosis of the novel.[39]

These writers are disruptionist in a number of ways. First, they see their immediate reality as a degraded manifestation of human values. Since it is a reality that has often been mythified for a variety of ulterior cultural and sociopolitical ends, they see Argentina and its all-consuming megapolis, Buenos Aires, as a project of demythification.[40] Medina emphasizes the *basurear* of human beings, especially women; Roffé underscores the worthlessness of traditional images of femininity and the "softening" touch of women; Lastra focuses on the gothicness of the ruling oligarchy; Puig emphasizes correlations between political and sexual oppression; Asís concentrates on the implications for the man in the street of the high-stakes fraudulence of long-standing ideological myths as embodied in one key political event.

Second, in these novels demythification assumes a variety of forms, from an apparently documentary image of things as they are but as few choose to recognize them (Asís's *Reventados*), to grotesque foregroundings (Medina's *Strip-tease*, Lastra's *Boca*), to overtly fictional postulates formulated in order to suggest an essential meaning (Puig's *Beso*, Corra's *Frontera*).

Third, language is perhaps the most notorious ingredient of these novels. There is little equivalent in the history of Latin

38. Indeed, the list of writers to fictionalize recent history alone would be extensive. In addition to Marta Lynch's novel analyzed in Chapter 4 of this study, reference should be made to novels by authors widely known outside Argentina, like Viñas's aforementioned *Cuerpo a cuerpo* and Puig's *El beso de la mujer araña*.

39. This is the sense in which Klinkowitz uses the term *disruptionist* in his *Literary Disruptions*. The point here is that the novel, by contrast to the purportedly objective mimesis of the interpretive social sciences, creates meaning by virtue of the semiotic patterns it develops. For an elaboration of these principles, see Michael Riffaterre, *Semiotics of Poetry*.

40. A comparison between the authors studied here and the Generación del 55, the so-called *parricidas*, is inevitable. Both share the need to demythify their national and urban reality, although the former do not share the *parricidas'* need to demythify explicitly their literary forebears. Both groups emerged during times of extreme turmoil and stringent censorship. See the Ph.D. dissertation by William H. Katra, "The Argentine Generation of 1955: Politics, the Essay and Literary Criticism."

American literature for the aggressive colloquiality of the novels that have been described in this study and the promotion of the writers they typify. There are many ways in which colloquial registers have been represented in Latin American literature, from the double axis of the regional and the rural in nineteenth-century *costumbrismo* (culminating in the phenomenon of the *literatura gauchesca*) to the texture of urban speech in writers like Roberto Arlt, Manuel Rojas, Luis Spota, Mario Benedetti, and Gustavo Sainz. But few writers have been able to make literature out of sociolinguistic registers that are usually dismissed as scatological or pornographic. For this reason, one cannot speak simply in terms of a language that reflects faithfully the nitty-gritty features of lower-class urban speech. Rather, it is necessary to stress how that speech involves a range of linguistic features that bespeak a range of experiences ignored or covered over by various mythificational processes: homosexuality, the world of raunchy flesh merchants, incest and other sexually exploitive phenomena, the underbelly of commercial enterprise. The novels of these writers are linguistically creative not because they invent verbal symbologies for these phenomena in a modernist sense, but because they have the audaciousness to break with overwhelmingly powerful taboos and to call them by their "right"—colloquial, quotidian—names.

Fourth, each of these novelists, despite strikingly divergent strategies, constitutes an alternative to the readerly novel that still prevails in Latin American fiction even two decades after the first convention-breaking onslaughts of the *nueva narrativa*. Although it is probable that each novelist, all too aware of what he or she is attempting to achieve against enormous odds, may feel uncomfortable about being grouped with the others in this study, the qualities of novelistic rupture discernible in their texts provide them with a common generational denominator. (Puig, to be sure, does not quite fit: fifteen years older than the youngest, Roffé, he lives abroad and has the privilege of seeing his country from afar and of publishing in Spain free from the restrictions of censorship.)

Novelistic rupture itself constitutes a formal element of demythification in that, by breaking with the conventions of a certain standard of comparison (the easily assimilable novel), a novel also by implication breaks with whatever vision it itself proposes. The patterns of rupture involved include the seeming documentariness of Medina's and Asís's novels, the intertextualities with subliterary forms (journalistic news reports and chronicles, pornography, photonovels, and a grab bag of low-grade verbal texts), juxtapositions of various discursive forms (narratives versus diaries, versus second-level narratives based on other cultural media in the case of Puig's novel), and a series of textual features that represent an implicit opposition to the plot-and-character-oriented novel (Corra, for example). Although the human beings that populate these novels are memorable in a negative sort of way, they are hardly the lovingly developed and profoundly redeeming individuals one finds in mythificational fiction.

It should come as no surprise that the works examined in this study are, to a large degree, extremely controversial in Argentina. Indeed, some are not as well known as my inclusion of them here might suggest simply because they have been banned or severely restricted (I am referring, of course, to the situation in Argentina before censorship was lifted in late 1983). Moreover, it is difficult to write in a completely objective manner about very recent fiction, particularly the fiction of a country that has undergone serious internal upheavals.[41] Fiction is a very protean form of literature, and current writing in the West subscribes to a deliberate blurring of margins separating fiction from nonfiction; "serious" from "camp," "popular," or "pulp" novels; "readable" fiction from "academic" pseudofiction (a distinction widely propounded by Gore Vidal, whose writing otherwise certainly exemplifies a nonnormative approach to narrative genres).[42]

Buenos Aires is a major literary and publishing center and is therefore a hotbed of competing *trenzas*, the "strands" of different power groups, ideologies, or normative positions. There is a classical strand in the Argentine novel that would insist that the *nueva narrativa* never existed or that it was highly overrated and that "solid" novels like those of, say, Eduardo Mallea have been overshadowed by the "pornographers." And it would be naive not to acknowledge that, given the recent sociopolitical climate in Argentina, only the politics of the literary supple-

41. See my study of some key novels published during the miltary dictatorship, "Narrativa testimonial argentina en los años del 'Proceso.'"
42. Concerning generic classification in contemporary literature, see Barbara Herrnstein Smith, "On the Margins of Discourse," Chapter 3 of her *On the Margins of Discourse: The Relation of Literature to Language*.

ment distinguish the writers who support and are in turn praised by official sectors from those novelists who write on the margin of the establishment.

Rigid classifications in the West concerning good versus bad literature or polished versus sloppy writing have given way to intense debate over whether it is even possible to establish aesthetic standards for literature.[43] As a consequence, a critic may be less concerned about how "well" a work is written than about what narrative processes it employs: even a work that, by my personal standards, is poorly written, may be well worth studying in terms of what it does do. After all, scholars study many works of early literature as important examples of specific genres, themes, or influences without having to acknowledge them as great or even successful works of literature.

Contemporary literature is rife with controversy over what is "literary." To dismiss certain works as not literary enough (which may be one way of saying they are bad literature) is to apply a normative standard that readers may wish to believe is universally applicable. Public discussions are plentiful in Argentina over why certain writers deserve condemnation: Puig writes thinly veiled pornography, Medina is sloppy stylistically and cannot plot convincingly, Juan Carlos Martini Real is pretentious in his choice of themes and situations, Marta Lynch is cynically ambiguous in her feminism and in her handling of recent sociopolitical turmoil, David Viñas should stick to political history since his novels are only transparent fictionalizations of social-science topics, Eduardo Gudiño Kieffer is opportunistic in his choice of popular themes of social alienation, Silvina Bullrich writes only for bored women who do not want to see too strong an image of themselves, and so on. In all, the spectrum of complaints is not much different than what one reads about contemporary U.S. novels in both wide-distribution and academic reviews. My point is simply this: while we may prize the cogent attempt to distinguish lasting works of literature from noble—or even ignoble—failures, we study contemporary literature for reasons other than determining whether we consider it good or bad.

Finally, there is the matter of who has been included and who has been left out of any study. Again, because Buenos

---

43. For a representative statement, see Frederick Crews, "Anaesthetic Criticism," in his *Psychoanalysis and Literary Process*, pp. 1–24.

Aires is a major publishing center, it is impossible even to refer to every novel that attracted notoriety in the seventies, and every critic will have a personal list of the most significant works. In the final analysis, the justification for the works included in the present study is their countercultural quality (with whatever "distortion" of Argentine fiction in the seventies this may imply) and the manner in which they represent something like a typology of sociocultural issues and narrative strategies. Only time—and a more extensive assessment than the limitations of a single chapter permit—will tell whether this is a reasonable choice of titles and a legitimate way of examining them.

4. Correcting the Balance: Varieties of Understudied Latin American Fiction

I

It is no longer necessary to advertise the fact that the contemporary Latin American novel is worthy of international stature, nor does the scholar need to list statistics of translations or English-language book reviews in order to prove that the writers of the new Latin American narrative have received international recognition. Of course, this recognition is not limited to the new narrative. Yet it is the latter that has inspired a certain rhythm of attention, whether because of the intrinsic quality of the works, the artful promotion of interested parties, or simply because the themes and forms of these writings have struck responsive chords among non–Latin American readers.[1]

Yet, despite the enormous bibliography of translations and criticism in languages other than Spanish—especially English and French—what has received recognition is only a fragment of the first-rate production available to speakers of Spanish and has had a baneful influence on academic criticism, which tends to focus narrowly on those figures considered internationally "hot."[2] Hence the rather disconcerting concentration of doctoral dissertations on Jorge Luis Borges, Carlos Fuentes, Julio

---

1. It is not possible to review here all the controversies concerning the boom and the question of the centrality or marginality of certain figures and works. The major journals and monographic publications are analyzed in David William Foster, and Luis Peña, "Materiales para el estudio de la nueva narrativa hispanoamericana: dos ensayos bibliográficos," *Revista interamericana de bibliografía* (to appear). The principal documentary studies are Emir Rodríguez Monegal, *El boom de la novela hispanoamericana, ensayos*, and Angel Rama, "El 'boom' en perspectiva."

2. As a consequence, though it is a valuable survey of writers who have attracted international attention, John S. Brushwood's *The Spanish American Novel: A Twentieth Century Survey* focuses on an array of best-sellers, with only passing references to other works.

Cortázar, Gabriel García Márquez, and a handful of others. The result is that, within the limitations of what can be taught in American programs of study, there is a disproportionate emphasis on only a few big names. As a consequence, it is difficult to grasp comprehensively the full range of contemporary Latin American fiction or its historical panorama.

In this chapter I propose to characterize, through the examination of sample texts, five trends that have received virtually no sustained critical attention: detective fiction, fictionalized accounts of contemporary political processes (perhaps the one category that is not strictly marginal, although again the focus has been on a few big names like Carlos Fuentes or Mario Vargas Llosa), erotic narrative, science fiction, and works written by "adult" novelists for children. Certainly, neither the works examined nor the categories into which I have grouped them have any privative value. My personal opinion is that, with very few exceptions (for example, Augusto Roa Bastos), the authors of the works studied here have been neglected by academic critics, despite the enthusiastic reviews accorded them in the journalistic or popular press. By the same token, my very broad typological classification is meant only to signal some of the varieties of fiction that I believe merit closer scrutiny and that might provide a more balanced assessment of the interests of both the writers themselves and their immediate, Latin American readers. Undoubtedly, anyone who reads widely in Latin American fiction can with little effort add categories and primary examples from among the large number of novels published every year in the major literary centers. By focusing on the few prime examples discussed below, I hope to encourage this sort of wider reading and appreciation of the very complex panorama of contemporary Latin American narrative that tends to be obscured by the concentration on a few internationally famous masters.

II

Jorge Ibargüengoitia (Mexico, 1928–1983) is not exactly a marginal writer: he is, to the best of my knowledge, the only Latin American novelist to win Havana's prestigious Casa de las América's prize on two occasions, once for his novel *Los relámpagos de agosto* (1965) and once for his play *El atentado* (1978). Nevertheless, despite the recognition and success he has had with his writing in terms of both sales and enthusiastic reviews in the mass-distribution press, little serious critical attention has been devoted to his plays and fiction.[3] This is no doubt due in large measure to the fact that Ibargüengoitia is only one of a large number of important contemporary Mexican writers whose work is overshadowed—at least among academic critics—by that of Octavio Paz, Juan Rulfo, and Carlos Fuentes. As important as recognition by literary supplements and general cultural publications may be for sales, they are no substitute for detailed critical analysis in assessing the long-range importance of a writer's work. The classic case in Mexican literature, of course, is Luis Spota: although he has been writing highly successful novels in a social-realist and neorealist vein for over forty years, authoritative critics have yet to accord him anything more than sporadic attention. This sort of imbalance continues to hinder the adequate assessment of modern Mexican writers by both national and foreign critics.[4]

By the same token, it is possible that critics accustomed to the dense magical realism of Rulfo's writings and the rather pretentious experimentalism of Fuentes's works are deceived by the apparent artlessness of Ibargüengoitia's fiction. If one of the abiding contributions of the boom writers of the sixties and early seventies was to make readers respect what Roland Barthes has called "writerly" literature—writing that resists immediate decodification and directs attention to its own semiological texture, a writing that Rulfo and Fuentes both exemplify—the reemergence of a seemingly transparent "readerly" writing leaves the critic who abhors interpretive reductionism, with its emphasis on the referentiality of the text, with nothing significant to say.

Ibargüengoitia makes use of two principles or strategies that give his texts the impression of facile "readerly" literature: an

3. See his autocriticism in "Memorias de novelas," *Vuelta*, no. 29 (1979): 32–34. An extensive analysis of *El atentado* is provided by John D. Bruce-Novoa and David Valentín, "Violating the Image of Violence: Ibargüengoitia's *El atentado*." See also the note by Gustavo García, "Jorge Ibargüengoitia: la burla en primera persona."
4. One important critical assessment of Spota's writings is by Walter Langford, "Luis Spota, Self-made Novelist," in his *The Mexican Novel Comes of Age* (Notre Dame, Ind.: University of Notre Dame Press, 1971), pp. 103–26. Of extreme significance is Carlos Monsivais's (unfulfilled) proposition: "Luis Spota: novelista del futuro," *Revista de la Universidad de México* 14, no. 5 (1960):37. Consult also Mauricio de la Selva, "Actualidad de Luis Spota," *Cuadernos americanos*, no. 204 (1976):225–35.

intertextuality with popular forms of para- or subliterature and flat urban colloquial registers that are disconsonant with the "poetic" language of magical realism and the self-conscious logophilia of the experimental "novels of language."[5] (Many of the latter make use of a heightened aggressive colloquiality, marked by the facetious wordplay and phatic tropes that in Mexico are lumped together under the term *albures*. José Agustín and Gustavo Sainz are two of the masters of this sort of writing, which parodies urban speech as an eloquent evidence of the contradictory and confused reality of its users.)[6] Ibargüengoitia, by eschewing both the poetic registers and the hidden reality of the experimental novels and by using a sociolinguistically revealing language, gives the impression that his writing is undifferentiated in style from the nonliterary texts.

Moreover, by working with generic codes reminiscent of the vast flotsam and jetsam of popular writing in Mexico (the country hosts a monolithic industry that exports to all of the Spanish-speaking nations of Central America and the Caribbean), Ibargüengoitia straddles the no-man's-land between Bellas Artes and the literature of the corner kiosk, a position that the popular writings of Luis Spota long ago showed to be a risky one. It is not so much a question of dignifying the popular genres, although the latter may be as socioculturally valid as those of the most internationally renowned novelist if read with appropriate analytical conventions.[7] Rather, the project exemplified by Ibargüengoitia in Mexico, along with Manuel Puig in Argentina, Luis Rafael Sánchez in Puerto Rico, Mario Vargas Llosa in Peru, Juan Marsé in Spain, and many others, is that such generic codes, by virtue of their identification with the broad spectrum of national or regional culture, offer potentially powerful strategies for postmodernist literature and its emphasis on disruptive, ironic, and contradictory semiologies.

One of the most successful forms of intertextual writing in Ibargüengoitia's fiction has been the detective or mystery novel.[8]

5. On the importance of this sort of language in the contemporary novel, see David William Foster, "La problemática del lenguaje en la nueva narrativa: observaciones liminares," and Lisa Block de Behar, *Análisis de un lenguaje en crisis*.

6. See Jorge Ruffinelli, "Código y lenguaje en José Agustín," *La palabra y el hombre*, no. 13 (1975):57–62.

7. An overview of this writing in Spanish is provided by Francisco Alemán Sainz, *Las literaturas de kiosko* (Barcelona: Planeta/Nacional, 1975).

8. The only study on detective fiction in Mexico is Donald A. Yates's essay on some rather unexciting imitators of foreign models, "The Mexican Detective Story," *Kentucky Foreign Language Quarterly* 8 (1961):42–47. Detective novels have been one of the most popular genres of fiction in Latin America. Thanks

In both *Las muertas* (1977) and *Dos crímenes* (1979), murder is the central event, and the analysis of its sociological implications serves as the dominant point of departure for the elaboration of the text. In a study by Angel Rama on the documentary writing of Rodolfo Walsh, as well as other contemporary examples of nontraditional and "subversive" literature—subversive to the extent that it challenges the canons of established or academic standards—Jorge Ibargüengoitia is the only Mexican writer that Rama notes to be within the scope of his study.[9] *Las muertas* is a paradigmatic example of Ibargüengoitia's place in such a context, not so much because *Las muertas* is documentary (although it could well be based on an actual event, such a distinction is not especially pertinent), but because of the novel's identification with an entire range of postmodernist fiction in Latin America that seems to lack a clear "literariness" because of its separation from the dominant magical realism promoted by the boom of the *nueva narrativa*.

Las muertas is the re-creation through flashbacks, in the best tradition of the police inspector's patient accumulation of bits and pieces of circumstantial information, of a scandalous re-

to the influence, through mass-distribution translations, of seminal and derivative works by American, British, and French authors and to the talents of Latin American followers and imitators, the formulas of detective fiction have been developed during approximately the last fifty years. Undoubtedly the most influential foreign writers have been Dashiell Hammett and Raymond Chandler, whose uncompromising portraits of the tattered social fabrics behind their crime plots echo the concerns of social realism and other forms of critical commentary in both the United States and Latin America. Chandler in particular struck a responsive chord in Argentina, where he was well represented by Spanish translations, and there are affinities between the pilgrimage of his protagonist "down all these mean streets" and the representations of modern humiliations in the works of Roberto Arlt and his literary heirs. Mexico's Vicente Leñero (*Los albañiles*, 1963), Uruguay's Carlos Martínez Moreno (*Tierra en la boca*, 1974), and Argentina's Manuel Puig (*Buenos Aires affair*, 1973) are only some of the prominent writers who have used the conventions of detective and crime fiction for the structural framework of narratives that are, in the final analysis, predominantly concerned with investigating and revealing social conditions. See Francisco Gaizón Céspedes, "Cuba: el papel del género policiaco en la lucha ideológica," *Casa de las Américas*, no. 89 (1975):159–62; and Rogel Ordóñyez, "La literatura policíaca en Cuba," *Areíto*, nos. 19–20 (1979): 64–65. There has been considerable Argentine scholarship on the subject: Jaime Rest, "Diagnóstico de la novela policial," *Crisis*, no. 15 (1974):30–39; Jorge B. Rivera, and Jorge Lafforgue, ". . .Literatura policial en la Argentina," *Crisis*, no. 33 (1976):16–24; Jorge Lafforgue and Jorge B. Rivera, "Historia: la narrativa policial en la Argentina," in their *Asesinos de papel* (Buenos Aires: Calicanto, 1977), pp. 13–67. Structuralist opinion like that of Tzvetan Todorov encouraged other academic interest in the detective genre: "Typologie du roman policier," in his *Poétique de la prose* (Paris: Editions du Seuil, 1971), pp. 55–65.

9. Angel Rama, "Rodolfo Walsh: el conflicto de culturas en Argentina."

venge by a whorehouse madam against a man who chose not to heed her attentions toward him. With a sense of humor both macabre and ironic that serves to comment implicitly on the details under scrutiny as well as to insinuate the sordid triviality of the lives that suddenly mesh to unleash the fateful chain of events, the novel probes the antecedents, values, aspirations, and venal motives of the participants in and witnesses to the crime, which takes place in a God-forsaken village in the interior of the country.

By making use of segments of narrative that are ostensibly reports by witnesses and declarations taken down from participants, the novel constructs a mosaic of the dead-end lives of these marginal individuals. The narrator's ironic framing obliges us to read these statements both as fragments of evidence in the emerging pattern of events and as unwitting characterizations of the unheralded emotions of social outcasts that erupt so violently against themselves:

> Durante su reclusión en la cárcel Simón Carona relató el caso de Ernestina, Helda o Elena de la siguiente manera:
>
> La vi venir caminando entre árboles de la alameda y no lo quise creer. Aquella mujer vestida de negro con la bolsa de charol en la mano no podía ser Serafina. Se parecía a ella y se vestía como ella pero no podía ser ella. De todas maneras sentí que me temblaban las rodillas. ¿Será que todavía la quiero?, pensé.
>
> Yo estaba parado afuera del quiosco de la nevería esperando que dieran las doce para ver a un señor de la Oficina de Hacienda con quien tenía que hablar para que me perdonara unos impuestos. La mujer seguía caminando entre los árboles y mientras más se acercaba a mí más se parecía a Serafina. No puede ser ella, volví a pensar para tranquilizarme: vive en otro pueblo, no tiene a qué venir a Pajares. Ella seguía caminando y acercándose, creyendo, me dijo después, que el hombre que estaba parado afuera de la nevería no podía ser yo. Cuando alcancé a verle los pómulos salientes, los ojos negros rasgados y el pelo restirado era demasiado tarde. Era Serafina y me tenía acorralado.
>
> Ella fue derecho a donde yo estaba, abrió la boca como si empezara a sonreír—alcancé a verle el diente roto—y me dio la bofetada. . . .
>
> Fui caminando por las calles chuecas de aquel pueblo, al rayo del sol y entre las moscas, porque era junio, diciéndome a mí mismo: "todavía te quiere, la prueba es que te dio la bofetada".[10]

10. *Las muertas*, pp. 16–17. The translation is taken from *The Dead Girls*, trans. Asa Zatz, pp. 15–16. Further citations from both will be made by page number in the text.

(Following is the case of Ernestine, Helda, or Elena as told by Simón Corona while in prison:
I saw her through the trees in the square walking in my direction but didn't want to believe it. That woman in black carrying the patent leather purse couldn't be Serafina. She looked like her and was dressed like her but it couldn't be her. Whether it was or not, I felt my knees begin to tremble. Could it be possible that I am still in love with her? I asked myself.

I was leaning against a pole next to the ice cream stand in the square waiting for it to be twelve o'clock, the hour I had to see somebody in the Treasury office about a tax matter. The woman kept coming through the trees and the closer she got the more she looked like Serafina. No, it can't be her, I said to myself again just to calm my nerves. She is living in another town. There is no reason for her to come to Pajares. She was getting closer and closer, thinking, she told me later, that the man by the ice cream stand couldn't be me. When I was finally able to make out those high cheekbones, the slanty black eyes, and that hair pulled back tight, it was too late. It was Serafina, all right, and she had me cornered.

She came straight over to where I was, opened her mouth as if she was going to smile—I just caught a glimpse of that broken tooth of hers—and slapped me in the face. . . .

I walked through the crooked streets of that town with the sun beating down, the flies pestering me—it being June—and saying to myself, She still loves you. That slap in the face proves it.)

As the narrative texture of these reported declarations from essentially nonverbal individuals reveals, the novel attempts through its structure to capture the journalistic primacy of fact and circumstance. The dominant criterion is the belief that meaning or interpretation arises from the accumulation and juxtaposition of details rather than from overt exegesis. The details involved are reminiscent of detective fiction, the *fotonovela*, and the soap opera (the story of the spurned woman is, of course, only a particularly outrageous reworking of the many popular narratives typified by these genres). Yet, at the same time, Ibargüengoitia's narrative unquestionably parodies and satirizes the institutionalized and fossilized forms of discourse exemplified by these genres: if popular narratives are unconscious parodies of elite forms of discourse (for example, in ludicrous attempts to be poetic in amorous dialogue or to speak with the sociolects of authority in adventure stories), the sort of fiction represented by *Las muertas* parodies in turn its popular subtexts.

Thus, Ibargüengoitia's novel is characterized by a narrative focus that is "free-floating" to the extent that it does not specify a privileged point of view or set of values. It moves easily from the transcription of incriminating reports and statements by witnesses to the analysis of preverbal states of consciousness that underlie the impetuous and startling behavior of the characters in the drama being reconstructed. Moreover, there is a shuffling together of disparate texts, including items of information concerning Mexican sociopolitical customs after the fashion of A. Jiménez's famed *Picardía mexicana*, tidbits on how to run a model brothel in peace and quiet for twenty-five years, and advice on how to set up and execute a vicious revenge against a disdainful lover. The result is a narrative that moves with ease from one topic to another in adherence to the controlling principle of the mosaic accumulation of fact and circumstance. This strategy, which allows the superficial reader to assimilate the text in terms of the relatively brief narrative segments that seem to have only a tenuous interrelationship, introduces nuclear texts that bear directly on the macabre event under reconstruction, the brothel as a microcosm of an arbitrary and degrading social fabric:

En vez de que los ánimos se calmaran, al día siguiente de los "castigos ejemplares" ocurrió otro acto de insubordinación.

Fue así: Marta Henríquez Dorantes, la otra mujer que tenía permiso de salir de la casa acompañando a la Calavera al mercado, estaba en los lavaderos exprimiendo su ropa, cuando se dio cuenta de que varias de sus compañeras se habían acercado y estaban alrededor de ella, en silencio, y sin hacer nada que justificara su presencia en aquel lugar.

Estaba apenas dándose cuenta de estas circunstancias cuando las otras se echaron sobre ella. Como eran cuatro la dominaron fácilmente. La tumbaron al piso, la amordazaron y la ataron con la ropa húmeda que acababa de lavar, la hicieron levantarse y estuvieron a punto de darle una muerte extraña. En un rincón del corral había un excusado común antiguo que estaba en desuso desde hacía muchos años. Las mujeres llevaron a Marta arrastrando hasta esta construcción, quitaron las tablas del común e intentaron meterla en el agujero. (Por las descripciones de este hecho se deduce que las atacantes tenían intención de enterrar viva a la víctima.) Su gordura la salvó. Marta es una mujer de osamenta muy ancha y por más esfuerzos que hicieron las otras no lograron hacerla pasar por el orificio. Estaban en el forcejo cuando llegó la Calavera.

En esta ocasión no hubo castigo, sino separación. Las Baladro decidieron que las cuatro mujeres que habían atacado a Marta fueran llevadas al rancho Los Ángeles y encerradas en la troje, mientras que las cuatro que habían atacado a Rosa fueron encerradas cada una en su cuarto, con un candado en la puerta.

Por considerar que cuatro mujeres aisladas justifican montar guardia en las noches, el capitán Bedoya hizo que a partir de la siguiente, un soldado de confianza—el Valiente Nicolás—se quedara en el Casino del Danzón, armado, y estuviera a las órdenes de las Baladro, en caso de que algo se ofreciera. (pp. 138–39)

(Instead of things settling down after the "lesson," another act of insubordination occurred.

Marta Henríquez Dorantes, the other woman who was allowed to leave the house to go to market with the Skeleton, was in the laundry shed wringing out clothes when she realized that several of her companions had entered and were standing around her, in silence, doing nothing that would explain why they were there.

She barely had time to become aware of their presence before they jumped her. Being four, they overcame her easily. They threw her to the floor, gagged her, and tied her arms and legs together with the wet clothes she had been washing, stood her up, and tried to kill her in a strange manner. There was an old outhouse in a corner of the yard that had been in disuse for many years. The women dragged Marta to this building, removed the boards covering the hole, and tried to stuff her into it. (The description of this deed leads to the conclusion that the attackers intended to bury their victim alive.) Her fatness saved her. Marta is a very broadly-built woman, and no matter how hard they tried, her assailants were unable to push her through the opening. They were engaged in the attempt when the Skeleton arrived.

This time the women were not punished, they were segregated. The Baladros decided that the four who had attacked Marta were to be taken to Los Pirules farm and shut up in the barn and the four who attacked Rosa should be locked in their rooms.

Considering that holding four women in solitary confinement called for vigilance during the night, Captain Bedoya assigned a trusted altern—Brave Nicolás—to stand guard, armed, and be at the orders of the Baladros in case anything came up.) (p. 116)

It should be evident that Ibargüengoitia belongs to a neo-realist strand of the contemporary Mexican novel that is interested in documenting the unsavory details of a society whose daily reality is far removed from the self-serving myths of the ruling political machine. But his pseudodocumentary style (pseudo because, unlike the texts studied in Chapter 1, *Las muertas* does not depend on the readers' identification of an actual event or on the narrative presence of a historically real individual) refutes modernist literary artifices and stands as far removed from the novels of Carlos Fuentes (in which it is the lack of ironic humor that fails to distinguish between what is important and what is trivial and, therefore, in which the norm is a "poetic" fiction) as it does from those of José Revueltas and Luis Spota.

In the case of the novels of Revueltas and Spota, the implacable emphasis on the festering wounds of Mexican life obviates the need for any sardonic or analytic commentary. As in the works of other contemporary Latin American writers who deal in postmodernist semioses, the ironic distancing imposed by Ibargüengoitia's narrative strategies situates the reader between the much-vaunted conventions of narrative art and the cultural codes of the marginated individuals the novel proposes to study. In coordinating these diverse narrative points of reference, the reader must make the transition from assimilating an apparently artless, "readerly" text to assembling a coherent pattern of significant meaning from the fragmentary narrative the author provides.

* * *

Contemporary Brazilian narrative is one of the most exciting in Latin America. It is as though all of the years of censorship and violent repression that followed the fateful military coup of 1 April 1964—the first of the self-righteous "cleansing" coups by the military in one after another of the major Latin American countries during the past twenty years—induced a fallowness of creative talent in Brazil that erupted in a series of significant publications under the relative freedom (almost unique on the continent at the moment) of the first half of the 1980s. This period of open expression has coincided with the postboom in Spanish America and with the postmodernist repudiation of the primacy of the "literary" artifact.

Brazil's major contemporary novelist and that country's prime participant in the boom, João Guimarães Rosa, who died in 1967, and the novelists who have emerged since 1975 manifest the same disruptive attitude toward vanguard literary canons that we find in the writings of Manuel Puig or Jorge Ibargüengoitia. Roberto Drummond, Rubem Fonseca, and Luiz Fernando Emediato are some of the pacesetting authors whose work reflects the dominant postboom and postmodernist criteria prevailing in Latin America, with emphasis on charting the continuity between traditional literary forms and the overall cultural discourses of a society, on demythificational procedures vis-à-vis establishment institutions and value systems, and on discovering in the colloquial language the basic models for their narrative texture. Although modalities we can generally associate with the poetics of magical realism continue to exist in Brazilian fiction, the use of macroforms—and ones traditionally considered "nonliterary"—like science-fiction, detective fiction, pornography, and the adventure story is notable among writers who have emerged since the seventies.

One recent and important example of the use of crime fiction, although in a fashion significantly different from Jorge Ibargüengoitia's *Las muertas*, is Miguel Jorge's *Veias e vinhos* (published in 1981 by one of the newer and more innovative publishers, Editora Ática of São Paulo). While military governments continue to prevail in other major literary countries like Argentina (at least until late 1983), Chile, and Uruguay, Brazil now has a civilian government; as a consequence, Brazilian artists are among the few on the continent who may call things by their proper names.[11]

Jorge's novel would not have been possible even ten years earlier because of its frank and explicit treatment of an issue of social concern. *Veias e vinhos* is a crime novel that deals with an apparently true incident in Goiânia in the mid-1950s (although it does not qualify as a documentary novel since there is no explicit use of nonfictional texts): the parents and four children of a family are beaten to death during the night. The only witness and survivor is the youngest child of the family, a little girl barely able to utter a few words. Neither the motive for the crime—it appears to have been the work of hired assassins— nor the identity of the killers is ever officially established. Structured in segments that alternate among the life of the family in the few days before the murder, the actual crime as it is refracted in the preverbal consciousness of the infant, and the cynically incompetent police investigation of the crime, Jorge's narrative presents a complex mosaic of dialogues, interior monologues, and narrative transitions in a diversity of linguistic registers (including a prison argot that requires a lexical

11. Concerning censorship in Brazil and contemporary fiction, see Emir Rodríguez Monegal, "Writing Fiction under the Censor's Eye." The other side of the coin is presented by Robert Krueger, "Abertura/apertura: A Political Review of Recent Brazilian Writings."

appendix). Indeed, the jacket of the novel announces rather gratuitously that this is a work that revitalizes "natural" narrative in the Brazilian novel: the novel may not be an example of magical realism, but it is anything but a transparent, readerly story.

Like other modern writers who have seen in the circumstances of murder an allegory of social malaise, Jorge uses the crime his novel investigates as an opportunity for the depiction of marginal social existence and police corruption. It emerges that the family owns a small general store, an occupation that puts them in the center of a day-to-day economic system that barely provides for survival. The paterfamilias is caught between the demanding drudgery of his business and dreams of moving into Kubitschek's new fantasy city of Brasília, where he believes he will strike it rich in the Brazil of the future. He is an Everyman victim of the discontinuities between national myths of greatness and inescapable social realities; at the same time he is the point of reference for a scathingly ironic juxtaposition between an immediate reality and a grandiose ideal.

After the death of the family, the police—who are insinuated to have been the agents of the crime because of friction between their swaggering and bullying captain and the store owner—torture the latter's brother and business partner into confessing that he paid to have the crime committed. Thus, in addition to belying myths of prosperity, Jorge's novel does not hesitate to see in the judicial system, ostensibly charged with solving the murder and punishing the guilty parties, an exact image of the national hypocrisy.

Perhaps the most eloquent strategy of Jorge's novel—in addition to its use of overlapping fragments that echo and reecho the basic motives of the narrative, including the mother's symbolic dream in which a vulture foreshadows the subsequent murders—is the refraction of the carnage in the preverbal consciousness of the youngest member of the family. Her bewildered witness of an event that she can neither grasp nor interpret is a figure for the crime novel that, in the face of a corrupt judicial system that sacrifices truth and justice to political expedience, cannot in the final analysis "solve" the crime:

Demais eu disse: Sou Ana, que querem de mim? Cada vez mais, me olhavam, cada vez mais eu me enroscava no cortinado do berço. Eles me viam como se vissem uma fotografia, não era eu quem estava ali, não podia ser. Podia ter tentado conseguir que eles me matassem, mas não tentei, e por isso, um deles persistia nas palavras: "Você vai deixar esta escapar? Por quê? Deu cagaço?" Meus olhos seguiam as manchas de sangue sombreando o chão, e eu estava com uma chupeta velha e suja enfiada na boca, à moda de uma mordaça. Um dos homens me fez um gesto com a mão e eu me encolhi. Agora pareciam estranhos bichos, daqueles que me vinham em sonho e que me causavam pavor. Os olhos do pai cresciam e saíam do rosto e andavam vagando pelo quarto, sem poder sair, sem poder me ver, me acudir. Aqui, pai, aqui, eu estou aqui. E eles se voltam para mim, duas flores brancas, despetaladas e sem cor. Não importo que eles me fitam. Fitam-me e dizem alguma coisa. O quê? Me pergunto à toa. O quê? O quê? Seu corpo, no entanto, permanece no mesmo lugar, jogado por cima do corpo da mãe. Que beijo estranho seria aquele? As mãos caídas, os joelhos afastados, as bocas desunidas, e a noite rodando entre eles.[12]

(Furthermore I said: I'm Ana, what do you want with me? They kept looking at me more and more and each time I would wrap myself up more and more in the curtain of the crib. They looked at me like someone looks at a photograph, I wasn't the one who was there, it couldn't be. I could have tried to get them to kill me, but I didn't try. As a consequence, one of them kept saying: "Are you going to let that one off? Why? Did she make a fuss?" My eyes followed the bloodstains darkening the floor. There I was with an old and dirty pacifier stuck in my mouth, like a gag. One of the men made a gesture toward me with his hand, and I shrunk back. Now they looked like strange animals, like the ones that came to me in dreams and frightened me. Father's eyes grew and left his face and drifted around the room, without being able to leave, without seeing me, without coming to me. Here, father, here, I am here. And they turned to me, two white flowers, shorn of their petals and colorless. It doesn't matter that they are looking at me. They stare at me and say something. What? I ask myself in vain. What? What? His body, meanwhile, lies in the same place, flung across mother's body. What strange kiss is that? Hands hanging loose, knees apart, mouths separated, and night rolling between them.)

While the persecution of social revolutionaries and human-rights advocates continues to be an important concern of the

12. *Veias e vinhos*, p. 75. The novel is studied by Erilde Melillo Reali, "Tendências da nova narrativa brasileira: *Veias e vinhos* de Miguel Jorge," and José Roberto de Almeida Pinto, "Foco narrativo—discussão sobre a nomenclatura proposta por Coelho de Carvalho, à luz de um romance de Miguel Jorge [*Veias e vinhos*]." See the overview of Jorge's fiction by Wendel Santos, "Os quatro ângulos do quadrilátero: a idéia da forma e a forma da idéia em Miguel Jorge."

Latin American novel, novels like Jorge's that examine the mind-
less destruction of everyday citizens are even more frightening: the decent, law-abiding citizen may be convinced that
guerrillas are only getting what they deserve (the fate of the
Uruguayan Tupamaros, for example, or the Argentine Mon-
toneros). But there is no self-deluding explanation for the form
of "social justice" elucidated by *Veias e vinhos*. The structuring
of the novel around the void created by the lack of an adequate—and, therefore, comforting—explanation of the crime,
despite the array of complex narrative strategies, is what makes
it such an eloquent example of social testimonial.

III

With the possible exception of "fresh" revolutionary societies—Cuba in the early sixties, Nicaragua in 1979–1980,
even Chile in 1973—the image of unrelenting sociocultural
decline, of the entropy that mediates between ideals and the
texture of everyday life, is a constant in most Western literature. Argentina, a country that has been in social and political
shambles since the first military coup fifty years ago that ended
the myth of a strong Latin American liberal society, is no exception. As a consequence, the preoccupation with the impos-
sibility of an ordered existence in Argentina has not only been
one of the constants of that country's literary production but
has also been synecdochal of a concern for the relationship between individuals and their society throughout Latin America.

The problem for a writer seriously committed to recording in
acceptable literary structures the texture of recent Argentine
life has not been what image of society to project: the superficial details of national events have a way of imposing themselves on writers. Rather, the problem has been what semiotic
strategies to employ in working out a text that alludes to those
events and creates a system of meaning for them. Even more
significant is the question of how to write seriously about the
problem without having your novel banned and without en-
dangering your person. One of Enrique Medina's most recent
novels, published at a time when political chaos was even more
acute than is customary, is called *Las muecas del miedo* (1981) and
refers to the official and paraofficial use of frightening and startling gestures as a technique of repressive social control.[13] In

13. See my review in *World Literature Today* 56 (1982):309–10.

1981, Argentina had put behind it a period of street violence and massive guerrilla activity from both ends of the political spectrum. But only the naive were willing to believe that verbal dissent from the concept of Argentina propounded (no matter how inarticulately) by the ruling military and its supporters could be engaged in with constitutionally guaranteed impunity.[14]

Marta Lynch's novel *La penúltima versión de la Colorada Villanueva* (1978) is fascinating for its response to the challenge of how to publish in Argentina a novel dealing with recent political events. Lynch may well lament this assessment of her work. As Argentina's most renowned woman fictionist, she has established a considerable reputation for her evaluation of the role of women in Argentine society, with particular emphasis on psychological profiles of women attempting to come to grips with an existence in which they remain essentially marginal.[15] Like Lynch's other writings, *Colorada Villanueva* deals with a woman who feels she has lost control over events, feelings, and relationships. Lynch's success with the novel has been to bring together her interest in the roles of women and the questions of social dissolution in Argentina and to probe the interrelationships between the crisis of the individual and the crisis of a destructive sociopolitical process.[16] Abandoned by her family, with a husband who has accepted a teaching position abroad, a daughter caught up in guerrilla activity, and her loved ones dispersed by grim immediate realities, Colorada synthesizes individuals' loss of control over their own lives:

> Y en el medio de aquel cuerpo de medusa con seis brazos y seis piernas, dos cabezas despeinadas; en medio de aquel dios bicéfalo que se moviliza y se contrae, voces súbitamente alertas y enseguida armonizadas, un aire enrarecido estalla. No más pretextos. No más buñuelos tiernamente mixturados. No más canciones sobre la gui-

14. Concerning the difficulties for writers in Argentina, see Stephen T. Clinton, "Censorship, Human Rights under Videla." Of special interest in this regard is an article by Robert Cox, former editor of the *Buenos Aires Herald*, "Calling Terrorism by Name in Argentina," *Matchbox*, May 1982, pp. 2–3, 13. *Matchbox* is a publication of Amnesty International USA.

15. Basic studies on Lynch's writings are Martha Paley de Francescato, "Marta Lynch"; Naomi Lindstrom, "The Literary Feminism of Marta Lynch" and "Women's Discourse Difficulties in a Novel by Marta Lynch [*La señora Ordóñez*]"; Diane S. Birkemoe, "The Virile Voice of Marta Lynch"; and Monica Flori, "El mundo femenino de Marta Lynch y Elena Poniatowska."

16. Several dissertations have dealt with Lynch's interest in political issues. The most interesting is Amy Kaminsky's "Marta Lynch: The Expanding Political Consciousness of an Argentine Woman Writer."

tarra. No más charlas intencionadas alrededor de una mesa de café. No más llamados temprano, a la mañana. No más tiernas entrevistas en la calle. No más besos desesperados de los días sábados. No más. No más que el grito que escapa de la garganta del bicéfalo, un bicéfalo atacado por punzazos que agoniza. Yo, que he sido juez y testigo, agito por última vez estas tijeras. En paz también, consciente que ha llegado el tiempo de cobrar. Me cobro. La tijera punza muchas veces un cuerpo laxo ya, sin sangre, sin suspiros. Pero no hay nada que tomar de él, nada que alguien pueda condiciar. El hombre que amo no sirve para ceremonia alguna. Con dedos pringosos tomo su sexo, ese objeto minúsculo y casi cómico que, exangüe, se escurre a la presión. Presiono. Nada. No hay sangre que fluya, presión íntima que lo envalentone, efluvio que despierte este triste despojo que desaparece entre los pliegues de su pantalón. Por las piernas muertas, cae un objeto blando y de color negruzco, que perturbó mi vida consciente. Eso me arrancaba gritos (también a otras), me proveyó de vida, fructificó mi vientre por tres veces. Eso era una fuente misteriosa de placer y una provisión infinita de energías. Muere ahora. Desaparece. . . . Ya no más desventura. No más cálculos de horarios, ni detalles ni tampoco la ceguera parcial y necesaria ante el alto nivel alcanzado en el sufrimiento. Basta ya, Colorada, extendete, descansá.[17]

(And in the middle of that Medusa's body with six arms and six legs, two uncombed heads, in the middle of that bicephalic god which moves and contracts, suddenly alert and quickly harmonized voices, a rarified air, breaks out. No more pretexts. No more tenderly mixed rolls. No more songs played to a guitar. No deliberate chats over a café table. No more early morning calls. No more tender meetings in the street. No more. Nothing but the scream that escapes from the bicephalic's throat, a bicephalic attacked by jabs and now dying.

I, who have been judge and witness, wave these scissors for the last time. Also at peace, conscious that the time has come to get even. I take revenge. The scissors jab repeatedly at a body now limp, bloodless, sighless. But there is nothing to be taken from it, nothing anyone would covet. The man I love is worthless for any kind of ceremony. With grimy fingers I take his sex, that minuscule and almost comical object that, limp, shies way from my pressure. I press. Nothing. There is no blood that flows, no intimate pressure that embravens it, no flux that awakens this sad leftover that disappears among the folds of his pants. There hangs, between his dead legs, a blackish and soft object that unsettled my conscious life.

---

17. *La penúltima versión de la Colorada Villanueva*, pp. 193–94. Further citations will be made by page number in the text.

That thing that drew cries from me (and also from other women), gave life to me, fertilized my womb three times. That thing was a mysterious source of pleasure and an infinite source of energies. It is now dying. It is disappearing. . . . No more misfortune. No more juggling schedules, nor details nor the partial and necessary blindness either in the face of the high degree attained by suffering. That's enough, Colorada, stretch out, rest.)

Colorada's erotic, Molly Bloom–like interior monologue deals, of course, with one woman's agonizing sense of loss in her abandonment by a self-serving husband. Nevertheless, Lynch's novel makes it clear that the loss is far more than a personal drama and involves, rather, the breakdown of personal relationships in a society that seems unable to allow such personal luxuries.

Sociopolitical realities are omnipresent in Latin America, and Marta Lynch is one of the few serious contemporary writers in military-controlled Argentina (a country that has seen in the last ten years the crushing "mediocratization" of its culture) who could have published a novel that refers specifically and nonrighteously to the appalling carnage to which her country fell victim in the process of guerrilla warfare that raged from the early seventies to the end of the decade. In part because of her literary reputation, in part because of her recognition that any true humanitarian must wish a pox on both the left- and right-wing extremes (both were responsible for the carnage, although the latter enjoyed institutional support before and after the 1976 military coup and could count itself as much more "successful"), and in part—why not call attention to it?—because she has extensive connections with the ruling, industrial elite of the country, providing her with a protection not available to most writers, Lynch's novel has survived in the controlled marketplace of Argentine culture and received very favorable reviews from subtly different critical sectors.

How does Lynch address the crucial problem of providing a literary base for her portrait of an Argentine society violently coming apart at the seams during the explosive midseventies? *La penúltima versión de la Colorada Villanueva* is composed of brief untitled narrative segments and structured around events in the life of an upper-middle-class family during the space of a few months in late 1977. These events are perceived obliquely through the controlling consciousness (but not necessarily the first-person narrative) of Colorada, a forty-year-old woman who sees her family disintegrate around her without her being able to exercise any restraining influence—without being able to impose the matriarch's traditional authority over the family nest. At best, the protagonist witnesses herself losing control over the attentions and affections of her husband (he is a philosophy professor who accepts an appointment in Rio de Janeiro after being dismissed from his position in Argentina for vague political reasons) and her three teenage children (one separated from her husband and with a young child in tow, and two involved in rock-and-roll, drug culture as well as in dangerous political activities). Against the backdrop of a country experiencing daily crises, references to personal disasters with far-reaching emotional and psychological repercussions are punctuated by allusions to the Goyaesque slaughter of rival extremist factions, and one of Argentina's perennial myths—the sanctity of the family—is mercilessly dissected. The following passage describes the woman's attempt to adjust to absolute solitude after her abandonment by her loved ones:

La Colorada se viste ahora. No hay armonía en lo que elige para cubrir un cuerpo que experimentó cuanto la vida ofrece a una mujer normal, más joven por su aspecto que por la expresión adusta de su rostro triangular en el que se dibujan pasiones diversas; gusta de algo nuevo; la ironía. Siente la impresión de que está tomándose el pelo a sí misma en tanto elige una blusa blanca y unos zapatos comprados el día anterior. Debería saber la hora y descubrir también que la sensación que la acucia en ese momento es solamente de hambre. La noche de la víspera no ha querido prepararse comida alguna. No consiente en desayunar sola. Aprenderá a tomar su café en el bar y seguramente en pocos días tendrá la nómina completa de los que desayunan solos como ella. Ha recibido una carta de la fiel Dolores. Felipe es con la correspondencia extremadamente irregular. No ha vuelto a tener llamado de Ágata. Tiene tres hijos (uno por teléfono, de existencia dudosa, dos por correspondencia). Su marido no ha vuelto a sentir necesidad de telefonear. Ella pasa mucho de su tiempo en las confiterías, le encanta estar allí entre las parejas que discuten o se miran a los ojos. Le gusta mantenerse entre la mirada indiferente de los hombres y el tumulto (un confuso griterío de gaviotas) de las mujeres. Advierte que cada día se torna más y más invisible. Cuando se recompone, su invisibilidad disminuye pero sus ganas de ser puesta bajo observación son directamente proporcionales a su incapacidad para acicalarse. Es invisible pues y encuentra que tal condición novedosa no es mala. Por las noches, en el intenso silencio de su barrio, le parece escuchar algunas puertas. Suele ver también algunas fotografías nada borrosas aun con el paso del tiempo. Pero las puertas interiores, sobre todo, la mantienen adherida a un orden de acontecimientos a los que no puede renunciar. (pp. 357–58)

(Colorada is getting dressed now. There is no harmony in what she selects to cover a body that has experienced what life has to offer a normal woman, younger in her appearance than in the grim expression on her triangular face where various passions play. She enjoys something new—irony. She has the impression that she is making fun of herself while choosing a white blouse and some shoes bought yesterday. She ought to know the time and realize that the sensation that gnaws at her at this moment is only hunger. Last night she refused to prepare herself anything. She is unwilling to lunch alone. She will learn to have her coffee in the coffee shop, and surely within a few days she will have all the names of those who breakfast alone like she does. She has received a letter from the faithful Dolores. Felipe is extremely irregular about writing. She has had no further calls from Agata. She has three children (one by telephone, of dubious existence, and two by letter). Her husband has not felt the need again to phone. She spends a lot of time in pastry shops, and it pleases her to sit there among couples who argue or look into each other's eyes. She likes to hover between the indifferent stares of the men and the tumult (a confused chattering of seagulls) of the women. She has noticed that day by day she is becoming more invisible. When she shifts in her chair, her invisibility diminishes, but her desire to fall under scrutiny is directly proportional to her inability to fix herself up. Thus she is invisible, and she finds that such a novel condition is not bad. At night, in the intense silence of her neighborhood, she imagines she hears some doors slamming. She is also used to looking at some photographs that, despite the passage of time, are not at all fuzzy. But, above all, the inner doors keep her close to an order of events that she cannot renounce.)

In many respects, Lynch's novel is an elegant soap opera, and some readers may object to using the existential anguish of a comfortably situated suburban matron as the "historical" axis for representing one of Argentina's worst moments. In addition to the general human fear and trembling to which Señora Villanueva is subject because of her acute sense of alienation from both her personal and her political world, the novel contains abundant reminders concerning the secondary role of women to make the reader aware once again of the undercurrent of feminist consciousness in Lynch's writing. Despite the emphasis on margination and alienation as a general societal phenomenon that the individual has no control over, the protagonist's introspection concerning her role as a woman and mother is unmistakably prominent. (It must be noted that, in keeping with the economic integration of women in Argentina, Colorada is not an aimless member of society; by her own choice she is headmistress of a successful and exclusive private kindergarten).

Lynch's novel is, of course, not a soap opera, despite superficial resemblances with such texts. In place of the straightforward and readily accessible story characteristic of popular fiction, a complex texture is provided by an oblique narrative perspective that shifts temporally and spatially in order to chart patterns of events and reactions. Colorada Villanueva's point of view dominates but is not all-inclusive, and the inadequacy of any one perspective to sort out and explain the complex web of public and private occurrences is what provides the novel with its characteristic fuzziness. This quality is particularly evident in the several passages in which family photographs are verbally analyzed as basic points of reference in the novel.

The political theme never becomes very clear, it would appear by design. Lynch's sense of the horror is for the indiscriminate carnage, not for the persecution of any one political faction. The confusing elements of political strife in Argentina during the period are represented by the vague *ellos* to whom are attributed the failure of both the telephones and Colorada's personal emotional well-being. Of course, there are direct references to the bloodletting, and the description of the raid on a private apartment by right-wing thugs—who, in addition to beating up the occupants and carrying them off to a certain fate, also carry off the television, the telephone (still a luxury item in Argentina), and any other portable and salable valuables (pp. 284–91)—is counterbalanced by the senseless gunning down of Colorada's sensitive and humanitarian-minded brother-in-law, who is an army colonel.

While *La penúltima versión* is not a great novel, it is an important one. During a period of alarming sterility in Argentine letters, the fact that a writer would offer this version of recent national life bodes well for some degree of continuity with respect to the best aspects of national fiction.

* * *

Although the Uruguayan political process has not attracted the international attention accorded the Cuban revolution, the Allende phenomenon and the 11 September 1973 military coup, the Brazilian takeover of 1 April 1964, Perón's return to Argentina in June 1973, or the overthrow of Somoza in Nicaragua in 1979, the Tupamaro guerrilla activity of the late sixties and early seventies did attract some interest to the internal history of the much mythified "Switzerland of South America." Costa-Gavras's 1973 film on the Tupamaros, *State of Siege*, was in a sense the most prominent recognition of the events in Uruguay. Much has been written on the Tupamaros, but little on the political repression that has existed in Uruguay since the military assumed power in 1973.

Carlos Martínez Moreno's novel *El color que el infierno nos escondiera* (1981) is just one of many Uruguayan works to deal with that country's political process and the loss of innocence experienced by its citizens in the midst of economic collapse, the destruction of what for its time was an innovative and, by Latin American standards, highly successful form of government, and the emergence of a national way of life dominated by unyielding and violent repression. Martínez Moreno (1917–), who has a respectable inventory of novels to his credit dealing with institutional and structural violence in Latin American,[18] has written in *Color* one of the most important statements concerning the violent texture of daily life in one region of Latin America.

Dante's "Inferno" is understandably the best-known portion of the *Divine Comedy*: it is popular because it is the first part of the work, but also because it is the part that is primarily concerned with evoking the substance of an all-too-human world. Hell is nothing more than a highlighted image of our daily reality. Thus, in undertaking to evoke a sense of life in contemporary Uruguay, Martínez Moreno chose to take his title from Dante, as well as the epithets of the chapters and the mosaic structure of progression from one tableau to another.

The novel is initially halting because of a poorly handled account of an instructor of professional torture provided by the

---

18. See the studies by Emir Rodríguez Monegal, "Las ficciones de Martínez Moreno," and Mario Benedetti, "Martínez Moreno en busca de varias certidumbres."

United States government. It is a senseless caricature that is only worsened by ludicrous errors in detail about American life: children in Indiana probably don't even know what cricket is, much less play it, as the novel claims. However, the bulk of *Color* is a frighteningly faithful and well-controlled statement concerning both the extent of official violence perpetrated by "antiterrorist" regimes (with the help of their free-world mentors) and the ambiguities that besieged the Tupamaros in their attempt to pose a revolutionary alternative to Uruguay's drift toward dictatorship in the 1970s.

In terms of narrative strategies, *Color* is written from the perspective of ironic knowledge that the Tupamaros were wiped out and that there is no end in sight to the present dictatorship. In this sense, rather than projecting a historical awareness of the causes and repercussions of the movement, the novel becomes a meditation on coming to terms with a reality that one can never accept emotionally but that, because of its overwhelming presence, cannot be repressed:

> Un desaparecido político no va sustrayéndose gradualmente a nuestra presencia, como si fuera un ahogado en el inútil, frustráneo trance de salvarse. No hay remolinos en que una cabeza se sumerja, no hay turbiones en que un brazo aparezca y gire, no estamos—distantes e impotentes—asistiendo a una lucha donde él se pierda y con él su vida: un ahogado en la correntada de un río, un ahogado en la sobremesa de un picnic. Esa misma agua que lo guarda hasta mañana, que lo devolverá—edematoso, mordisqueado de peces—en el ribazo más plácido o enganchado a las rocas, no se lo ha llevado verdaderamente nunca. Siempre sabemos, aunque no dónde, aunque no cuándo. Allí estamos, anochece mientras caminamos a la orilla del río y atisbamos el horizonte cada vez más oscuro, y se hincha y se vuelve enorme e impenetrable la sombría masa del mar pero el náufrago es parte de su fauna y mañana podremos recogerlo. El desaparecido político de nuestras historias—en cambio—cae ya muerto desde su fábrica de tortura, desnudo, roto y mutilado a veces, ligado a un bloque de cemento o amarrado con alambres por pies, muñecas o rodillas. Puede haberse ahogado en una poza siniestramente pequeña, en el bidón del *submarino* donde se le haya echado a que se afixie o a que confiese, tanto da, no se sabe con cuál fin primordial, con qué objetivo verdadero. Si resiste y sale y en seguida declara, tal vez viva.[19]

19. *El color que el infierno me escondiera*, p. 203. See the review by Alfonso D'Aquino, "La novela que el cielo nos enviara."

(A person who has disappeared for political reasons does not re-
cede gradually from among us, as though he had drowned in the
futile and frustrating process of saving himself. There are no whirl-
pools in which a head submerges; there are no sharks into whose
mouths an arm disappears and twists around; we are not, distant
and impotent, witnessing a struggle where he loses and, in the process, loses his life. A man who drowns in the current of a river, a
man who drowns in the fun after a picnic. The very water that holds
him up until the next day, throwing him up on the most placid of
shores or wedging him among the rocks, edematous, nibbled at by
the fish, has never really carried him away for good. We always
know, although not where or when. There we are, dusk falls as we
walk along the banks of the river and watch the darkening horizon,
and the somber mass of the sea becomes bloated and enormous and
impenetrable. But the drowned man is part of its fauna, and tomor-
row we will be able to gather it in. The man who disappears for political reasons, on the other hand, falls already dead in his torture
factory, naked, broken, and often mutilated, tied to a block of ce-
ment or bound by the feet, wrists, or knees with wire. He may have
drowned in a sinisterly small hole, in the tub of the *submarine* where
he was held down so he would asphyxiate or confess, it's all the
same, for God knows what primordial object, for what real reason.
If he can stand it and resurfaces and tells them what they want to
know, perhaps he will live.)

In passages like the foregoing, Martínez Moreno juxtaposes
images of natural death—in this case, by drowning—and our
comfortable familiarity with them to images of death by torture, the death that has become the unnatural standard of Latin
American society. The novelist is careful enough (at least after
his opening chapter) not to present simply a partisan tract.
Rather, he uses the entire arsenal of contemporary narrative
strategies to provide a dense semidocumentary "revelation" of
a truly hellish social reality. Like Lynch's novel, *Color* testifies to
the extensive array of recent novels in Latin America that attempt to provide an adequate account of the repressive political
processes that, lamentably, have emerged as a continental norm.

IV

If truly erotic writing has never fared very well as literature
in the West,[20] it has been even less of a significant force in Latin

20. The recent monograph by Maurice Charney, *Sexual Fiction*, is a praise-
worthy attempt to analyze a group of "serious" erotic fictions.

American letters. Cuba's Severo Sarduy is probably the only major figure of the much touted new Latin American narrative to focus intensively on erotic themes. Other writers who have been censured for alleged obscenity or pornography cannot legitimately be identified primarily with the erotic. For example, Luis Rafael Sánchez in *La guaracha del Macho Camacho* (1976) uses the casually obscene or sexually explicit as one fragment of his comic mosaic of contemporary Puerto Rico. Manuel Puig utilizes the sexually graphic as part of his concern for the interrelationship between sexual repression and political repression and for the explosive violence that both generate. Only in *El beso de la mujer araña* (1976) does he come close to portraying the erotic as a complex and problematic form of expression and liberation, but in the final analysis his narrative is sidetracked by the greater political theme. I would venture to say that his concern for homosexuality, still a breath-catching taboo in his native Argentina, makes his novels seem more erotic than they really are. Gabriel García Márquez has some nice frankly erotic touches in *Cien años de soledad* (1967), but they are never developed. The majority of the texts collected by Enrique Jaramillo Levi in *El cuento erótico en México* are rather dreary, containing more purple-hued euphemisms than insouciant eroticisms.[21] I can think of no Latin American Georges Bataille or Henry Miller or Charles Bukowski, although Enrique Medina in Argentina comes close to the vision of the latter two American novelists.

If male authors and their narrators have yet to create an authentic erotic vision in Latin America, one would expect that the women authors, subject to even greater sociocultural restraints, would be even more circumspect on the subject. Yet the Latin American women writers who write unabashedly about erotic themes bear out the hypothesis that women artists may more effectively shatter such taboos and restraints because they are not of their own making but imposed on them by a male-dominated society. Argentina, which is certainly a sexually repressive society (or, to put it in less strident but no less ideological terms, a society enthusiastically supportive of the traditional Christian values of the chaste family), has produced some significant contributions in this regard. One recalls the

21. Enrique Jaramillo Levi, *El cuento erótico en México* (Mexico City: Diana, 1975).

scandal produced by Marta Lynch's *La señora Ordóñez* (1968), which opens with a woman's meditation on the sexual oafishness of her husband. And her *La penúltima versión de la Colorada Villanueva*, which I have already examined in this study, has the protagonist lamenting, as part of her loss of her husband, her interrupted sexual relations with him; part of the novel also concerns her degrading sexual adventure with a vacuous stud.

The protagonists created by authors like Reina Roffé, Cecilia Absatz, Silvina Ocampo, Luisa Valenzuela, and Susana Torres Molina all have sex drives that Argentine male authors have routinely denied their characters. I can think of only one major Argentine novel in which a woman's erotic needs are analyzed in depth in terms of both the repression of Eros and the oppression of women: Enrique Molina's *Una sombra donde sueña Camila O'Gorman* (1973). This novel retells the famous Camila O'Gorman story that occurred during the Rosas's dictatorship in the midnineteenth century, in which a priest and a highborn woman run off together. (Note should also be taken of José Donoso's 1980 novel, *La misteriosa desaparición de la marquesita de Loria*, also a respectable analysis of female sexuality in terms of societal conventions.)

For these reasons, the intrinsic quality of the writings of Mexico's María Luisa Mendoza is complemented by their importance as significant works by a woman writer on (among other things) female sexuality.[22] Of course, it would be a gross distortion to say that Mendoza's works are limited to questions of sexuality or eroticism; they are not. Mendoza, like most writers concerned with adequately representing sectors of society traditionally overlooked or marginated—in Latin America, in addition to women, these overlapping groups include homosexuals, the proletariat, indigenous cultures, and non-Christian minorities (Jews in particular)—focuses on a number of metonymic topics in giving voice to her characters, and only one of these topics is specifically erotic.

22. For an overview of Mendoza's work, see Charles M. Tatum, "María Luisa Mendoza, atrevida novelista mexicana." Of particular significance is the essay on Mendoza by fellow Mexican writer Rosario Castellanos, "María Luisa Mendoza, el lenguaje como instrumento." See also Grace M. Bearse, "Entrevista con María Luisa Mendoza"; Magdalena Maiz, "Tres escritoras: Garro/Castellanos/Mendoza"; and Dolly J. Young and William D. Young, "The New Journalism in Mexico: Two Women Writers [Mendoza and Elena Poniatowska]." Mendoza is included in the interviews by Elena Castedo-Ellerman, "¿Feminismo o femineidad? Seis escritoras opinan."

However, in *De Ausencia* (1974), Mendoza is directly occupied with an erotic theme. The story of Ausencia Bautista is not just the biography of a woman for whom sex is an integral part of her total personality.[23] Ausencia is a female Priapus, perpetually inflamed to the sexual possibilities of the world around her. Ausencia is a Priapus figure rather than a nymphomaniac because of her aggressive, assertive sexuality that shatters the traditional image of the submissive woman, who passively awaits the quenching of her sexual thirst by the dominant male. Ausencia as a virago inversion of sexual roles is only the first of many almost nonchalant ruptures with established cultural codes in Mendoza's novel.

Indeed, the immediate interest of *De Ausencia* derives from its systematic outrageousness in its portrayal of the heroine's movement through her sociocultural milieu. Ausencia is raised by her earthy father after the death of her mother in childbirth. A poor miner, he becomes wealthy through the discovery of a rich mineral vein, providing his daughter with the opportunity to transform his earthiness into her refined eroticism. Although Ausencia is educated by nuns, her personal view embraces a world of experiences of which they and her fellow townsman are completely ignorant. A child of nineteenth-century Mexico, Ausencia becomes a citizen of the silken world of underground Victorian, Byzantine fantasies[24]: her first lover is an adept New York Arab whom she and her Mexican peasant Romeo torture to death as an intense aphrodisiac adventure. Ausencia as the heir to her father's wealth is a respectable member of the decent ruling class, but she is also the regisseur of dramatic enactments of her all-consuming sexual fantasies. These are only some of the major ways in which Ausencia, symbolizing the closed Mexican society of the past, is also a sign for an erotic consciousness that is truly audacious in contemporary Latin American literature.

At one point in the novel, one of Ausencia's admirers is discoursing tediously about the tasteful details of a properly dressed Mexican man of society. Ausencia evades the assault of his boorish words by engaging in her favorite pastime, a fully

---

23. Charles M. Tatum has an excellent review of the novel in *Chasqui* 5, no. 1 (1975):54–55.

24. Ausencia undoubtedly evokes the characters in the writings studied by Steven Marcus, *The Other Victorians: A Study of Sexuality and Pornography in Mid-Nineteenth Century England* (London: Corgi, 1969).

elaborated sexual fantasy. As he prattles on about the attire-
ment of the body, Ausencia peels away layers of clothing to ar-
rive at her two choice fetishes: immaculately white underwear
and the glistening pubic triangle of hair it covers. The man,
noting her distraction, inquires: "—¿En qué piensas, reina, tan
allí traspasada por calladurías?" (What are you thinking about,
my queen, sitting there so transfixed by silence?")[25] She attempts to answer him, but he is incapable of grasping the sense
of her metaphoric speech or of intuiting the erotic fantasy her
words veil:

> —Caballero: mis nuevas propiedades para mí nada más. Es como
> por ejemplo usted, tú Reinaldo, aquí a mi lado, sin que yo te co-
> nozca, sin que sepa de ti más allá de tu idioma, y no obstante me
> estabas reservado. . . . Tú no sabes. Eres de la calaña que existe de
> las tres de la tarde en adelante, preocupado de tus propiedades que
> no habitas, como yo, y que significas en la ropa elegante, como si el
> smoking fuera respuesta. Pensaba yo en mis calladurías ¿entiendes?
> —No, preciosa, no entiendo. (pp. 102–3)

("Sir: my new properties are mine alone. It's as though you,
Reinaldo, here at my side, without my knowing you, without my
knowing anything about you except your language, and you had
been set aside for me. . . . You don't know. You are the kind that exists from three in the afternoon on, concerned about your properties you don't inhabit, like me, and what you mean in your elegant
clothes, as though your evening jacket were a response. And I
thought in my silence, Do you understand?"
"No, my sweet, I don't understand.")

Mendoza, in the details of the setting and contextualization
of her novel, makes abundant use of the hypothesis that Victorian culture was a sexually denatured exterior concealing an
intensely erotic subconscious, the Marcusian civilization versus Eros, or the Freudian superego versus the id. Using the circumspect Spanish of high literary fiction, Mendoza's narrative
voice articulates the *albur*, the vulgar and obscene Mexican
word play, that adequately characterizes Ausencia's removal
from the polite society of late-nineteenth-century manners
through which she distractedly moves.

But the reader, who may be interested only in knowing how
to explicitly describe sex in Spanish, should not make the mis-

---

25. *De Ausencia*, p. 102. Further citations will be given in the text by page
number.

take of reading *De Ausencia* as a joyful Dionysian romp through scenes of florid sexuality. It is true that Mendoza's stunning control over the linguistic possibilities of Spanish, her inventiveness at lexical bricolage, and her clever exercise of multiple stylistic registers give the impression that the novel belongs to the *Playboy/Playgirl* genre of sex as sniggering fun. The truly creative aspect of *De Ausencia* is its concern for the nostalgic frustrations of erotic fantasies, for how erotic fantasies are a sign for the individual's sense of loss, failure, unfulfillment. In a very Derridian sense, sex for Ausencia is an "absent center," both a lost meaning and an unattainable order. The fact that Ausencia can only pursue her erotic fantasies by repeatedly challenging the rigid norms of the prevailing social order and that their execution may involve the destruction of other human beings (she murders her Arab lover and spurns her Mexican lover, who is left with the blame for the disappearance of the former) is a major clue to the inherent limitations of her program of sensual self-expression.

As literary discourse, Mendoza's text is organized around the metaphor of the mirror. Each of the seven chapters is titled with a phrase referring either to a mirror (Primer espejo [First Mirror], Tercer azogue [Third Quicksilver], Cuarto trémol [Fourth Mirror Frame]) or to a trope for the basic mirror metaphor (Segundo reverbero [Second Shimmer], Quinto foco [Fifth Spotlight], Sexto reflector [Sixth Reflector], Séptimo lago [Seventh Lake]). Literary texts, to be sure, are often referred to in terms of a dead metaphor as "mirrors of life," and readers who are primarily interested in literature as a source of information concerning human society and individual experience are hardly violating the sense of art. Unlike those works of contemporary literature that question whether literature can adequately or accurately mirror life (for example, José Donoso's *El obsceno pájaro de la noche* [1970] or Mario Vargas Llosa's *Conversación en La Catedral* [1969]), Mendoza's use of the mirror as the controlling metaphor of her novel is primarily a sign for Ausencia's own narcissistic self-contemplation, both literally as she studies her body and works for its sexual fulfillment and to arrest its decay, and figuratively when she sees herself as the central character in the theater of her erotic fantasies.

The imperfection of the mirror, its distortions and its uneven quality, attests to the limitations of Ausencia's efforts at self-definition through erotic enterprise. One of her interludes is punctuated by strophes from a Gautier poem:

Cuánta nostalgia entre nos[sic] corazones
Tanto espacio entre nuestros besos
Amarga suerte. Dura Ausencia
¡Oh grandes deseos insatisfechos. . .! (p. 142)

(*What nostalgia between our hearts*
So much space between our kisses
Bitter luck. Harsh Absence
O grand unsatisfied desires!)

In the same passage, another Arab admirer reads the coffee grounds in her cup (another specular allusion):

Veo sangre que liquida las piedras en rojo, veo lenguas de saliva y un pozo sin dueño al que se le saca agua de mar que mata a las yerbas. Veo una desolación, una ausencia, una búsqueda sin cuento, sin encuentro, un sin fin de años congelados y muchas lágrimas, las aguas. . . (p. 145)

(I see blood that drenches the stones in red, I see tongues of saliva and a well without an owner from which one draws sea water that kills the plants. I see a desolation, an absence, an untold and unfulfilled quest, an endlessness of frozen years and many tears, the waters.)

Thus, far from being a portrait of female sexuality as a liberating force, *De Ausencia* is fundamentally concerned with how Ausencia's assertive erotic fantasies evolve into another form of physical and emotional imprisonment. Freed from the shackles of traditional Mexican repressive society, Ausencia enslaves herself to the elusive chimera of an unattainable erotic fulfillment. Like the heroines of Tennessee Williams's novel *The Roman Spring of Mrs. Stone* or Jean Rhys's *Good Morning, Midnight*, Ausencia's anagnorisis, the tragic discovery she must make in the mirror of her self-contemplation, is that destruction is the inevitable result of her feverish quest of sexual adventurism.

Mendoza's novel is characterized by an ample array of rhetorical strategies that we may call devices for reader distancing. It is a distancing that operates both for the reader interested in grasping Ausencia's tragic story and for the reader only interested in dwelling on the concrete details of her adventures as a Mexican Fanny Hill. The chronologically and therefore culturally remote setting (both Victorian Europe and traditional nineteenth-century Mexico so brilliantly represented in that great Mexican novel of repression, Agustín Yáñez's *Al filo del agua* [1947]), the use of a complex metaphoric or "baroque" narrative language, the intertwining of ironically witty observations with some of the hoariest clichés of pornographic writing, the development of complex patterns of dialogue and stream of consciousness: these are some of the textual strategies utilized by Mendoza to inhibit the reading of her novel as an erotic farce and, concomitantly, to encourage an appropriate contemplation of the essentially tragic image of Ausencia's sexuality.

De Ausencia is certainly not an Acción Católica denunciation of moral degeneracy or a call for a return to traditional sexual norms. But it is clear that, as a contribution to respectable Latin American literature dealing with women's issues and women's relationships to larger sociocultural questions, Mendoza's novel is a profoundly serious treatment of the problematics of erotic behavior. Hardly a document in favor of sexual repression, *De Ausencia* is a brutally frank and often outrageous representation of the tragedy of eroticism and its role as an aspect of adequate human self-fulfillment.

V

It is noteworthy that, while many Spanish-language novelists have written science fiction, especially in Mexico and Argentina,[26] the effort seems to be concentrated in Brazil, where writers like André Carneiro, José J. Veiga, Rubem Fonseca, and Ruth Bueno have made major contributions to a genre that moves uneasily between surrealistic fantasy and trenchant social commentary.[27] Significantly, science-fiction writing in contemporary Brazilian literature only rarely addresses the issues of technology that characterize the mainstream of American science-fiction writing. Rather, writers like Ursula LeGuin or

26. See the article by Ross Larson, "La literatura de la ciencia-ficción en México," and the anthology *Cuentos argentinos de ciencia-ficción* (Buenos Aires: Merlín, 1967). See also Marvin d'Lugo, "Fruto de los 'frutos prohibidos': la fantaciencia rioplatense."
27. With regard to science fiction in Brazil, consult the dissertation by David Lincoln Dunbar, "Unique Motifs in Brazilian Science Fiction." Moacy Cirne provides a checklist of works in his "FC: A/Z."

Ray Bradbury have been among the primary American models, fundamentally because of their search for alternative modes (itself an inheritance from surrealism) of representing human consciousness and values and for definitions of the crises of human society in terms that transcend the immediately historical.

If these writers are exponents of Robert Scholes's homophonous anacronym—SF for him means science fiction as well as structural fabulation, the sort of fictive writing the former anticipates in the postmodernist novel[28]—there can be little doubt that Brazilian writers see in science fiction a range of narrative modes that permits a critical commentary on social issues outside the framework of national myths and local color that continues to characterize much Brazilian writing. Jorge Amado remains the quintessential Brazilian novelist, and from Mário de Andrade's *Macunaíma* (1928) to João Guimarães Rosa's *Grande sertão: veredas* (1956) the mainstream of vanguard fiction in Brazil has remained intensely nationalistic. Science fiction offers a fertile alternative to this tradition and serves as a respectable counterweight to the quasidocumentary literature of social denunciation and demythification that has emerged in Brazil with the relative relaxation of censorship in the last ten years.

Rubem Fonseca's short story "O exterminador" (this is its original title, but it was included in his collection *Lúcia McCartney* [1969] with the title "O quarto selo [fragmento]") is a superb example of the melding of science fiction and social commentary, in this case on the secret police of repressive societies. I have written elsewhere that:

> [This story] is a sort of pseudo-science fiction tale concerning a terrorist operation set at some undefined future time to exterminate a Governor General. Written in ten relatively brief sections in a matter-of-fact tone that lends the text the appearance of a bureaucratic report, the story describes the initiation of the terrorist plan, the attempt by the Governor General to abort the plan, which has come to his attention, the terrorist-inspired street-rioting in the ghettos of Copacabana and Ipanema, the torture of one of the terrorist leaders, and the final assassination of the Governor General by one of the exterminators, the very man appointed to head the counter-terrorist operation.[29]

28. Robert E. Scholes, *Structural Fabulation: An Essay on Fiction of the Future.*
29. David William Foster, "The Brazilian Short Story," p. 28.

André Carneiro (1922–) is perhaps Brazil's most respected science-fiction writer, and he is the author of an important essay on the genre in which, after rejecting the unjust ways in which it is repudiated as escapist literature, he underscores its pertinence to the mainstream of serious narrative.[30] *Piscina livre* (1980) is one of Carneiro's notable contributions to science-fiction literature, and there is no question that it fulfills the goal of structural fabulation to interpret a sociocultural circumstance via the conceitful and often extravagant metaphors of contemporary fiction. The novel focuses on a variant of the modern theme of dehumanization: man's fear of being displaced from the center of the ethical and social order by robots. That such robots may be the most effective instruments of a repressive political order lends the topic a special relevance for Latin American authors and their readers in their concern for understanding the "unhuman" exercise of arbitrary power and the techniques of dictatorial regimes to maximize their control over a "robotized" citizenry.

One of technological man's recurring mythic nightmares is the takeover of the robots, as in Karel Čapek's expressionistic masterpiece, the drama *R.U.R.* (1920; the acronym stands for Rossum's Universal Robots). Carneiro explores the revolt of the humanoids in a harmonious technological world. It is a world built on profound sensual gratification (in reference, undoubtedly, to the inherent qualities of the consumer society) but devoid of a coherent recognition of the mystery, the poetry, the neuroses that seem to define essential humanness—that is, it is a world in which art and its abiding concerns have been repressed. The perfect world of the future, served by the humanoids who are masters of erotic pleasure, has no room for "antiquated" emotions and uncertainties. It is the perfect realization of the New Order so stridently touted by the architects of the Latin American revolutions of "liberation," the "recovery of the fatherland," and the "new" Argentina, Brazil, Chile, Uruguay, or wherever.

Significantly, it is the humanoids in *Piscina livre*, robots made in the questionable image of man, who organize a revolt against domineering mankind. To do this, they must circumvent the

---

30. Carneiro's essay is entitled *Introdução ao estudo da ciência ficção*. On his own writing, see the entry under his name by Leo Barrow in David William Foster and Roberto Reis, *A Dictionary of Contemporary Brazilian Authors*, pp. 30–31.

Central Computer, a machine like them but programmed to serve anthropocentric man:

O Computador Central, pai bondoso e justo ou ditador implacável e todo-poderoso, estava calado diante da situação. Não deu ordens nem pediu audiências. Consultado, deu respostas misteriosas e evasivas, onde as palavras Andrs ou Homens eram evitadas, como se não houvesse duas facções e um clima de expectativa e desordem, desconhencido há muitas décadas. Os serviços coletivos dependiam dele. Niguem se lembrava de que o movimento dos rolantes, a abertura das cúpulas, o condicionador de climas, o controle dcs alimentos, a energia para as casas funcionarem nasciam do Computador. Ele era uma coisa óbvia, como o crescimento de uma árvore, o vento tocando as nuvens. Olvidava-se que sem ELE todo o mecanismo pararia e o homem regrediria séculos. Isso era uma tolice, como se pensar que uma árvore parasse de fabricar seiva e folhas para se vingar dos insetos abrigados no seu tronco. Todos continuaram a viver, como se o mundo tivesse sido sempre imutável e imperturbável.[31]

(The Central Computer, a bountiful and just father or implacable and all-powerful dictator, remained silent in the face of the situation. It gave no orders, nor did it request audiences. Consulted, it gave mysterious and evasive replies, where the words Andrs or Men were avoided, as though there weren't two factions and a climate of expectation and disorder, unknown for many decades. The collective services depend on him. No one remembers that the movement of the rollers, the opening of domes, the air conditioners, the control of foods, the energy that allowed the houses to function all came from the Computer. He was an obvious thing, like a tree growing or the wind touching the clouds. One forgot that without HIM, the whole mechanism would stop and man would regress centuries. That would be folly, just as if one were to think a tree could stop producing sap and leaves in order to avenge itself against the insects taking refuge in its trunk. Everyone had continued to live as though the world had always been immutable and imperturbable.)

Carneiro's novel blends standard science-fiction conceits—the defamiliarization of what our modern world takes for granted, the normalizing of what we still see as outrageous (completely uninhibited sexuality and the technological perfection of bureaucratized prostitution), and audacious interpreta-

31. *Piscina livre*, p. 119.

tions of symbolic motifs (sex as a form of mind and body control rather than as the personal act of liberation we tend to see it as at the present moment). These conceits are elaborated with structural procedures that characterize the postmodernist novel—narrative fragmentation, "disruptionist" transitions from one event or circumstance to another, and understated symbologies that leave the reader at a loss for the immediate significance. For example, there is presumably some significance to the fact that the humans have a new name assigned each day by the Central Computer, while the humanoid Andrs have fixed names that imply the bygone days of human personality as a complex but fixed matrix of behavioral and psychological features.

Piscina livre (the title refers to the legalized brothel in which the human protagonist meets the humanoid prostitute who becomes her lover while pursuing his guerrilla operation against the Central Computer) is a rather transparent allegory of lost humanness in the brave new world of the future, of lost humanness in the New Order of an efficient fascist dictatorship. But it is certainly an eloquent example of the use by contemporary Brazilian novelists of the expressionistic possibilities of science fiction to comment on very real immediate sociocultural issues. In this sense, by using a nontraditional genre like science fiction writers can strive for the more intense concentration of meaning that is the goal of all defamiliarizing and experimental modes of fabulation.

* * *

Ruth Bueno has asserted that her novels may seem highly lyrical because she is a frustrated poet.[32] Yet the suggestive nonverisimilitude of much of the prose of *Asilo nas torres* (1979) is less lyrical (in the sense of comforting subjectivism) than it is Kafkaesque and alienating. Bueno's fifth work of fiction may best be classified as science fiction, and the icy whiteness of the landscape in *Asilo* is similar metaphorically to the wintry terrain of Ursula K. LeGuin's classic, *The Left Hand of Darkness* (1969). Science fiction in this context means not surreal technology but the nonnaturalistic or defamiliarizing metaphor of the unknown, the yet-to-come, and the still-to-be explained.

32. See the entry on Bueno by José Afrânio Moreira Duarte in Foster and Reis, *Contemporary Brazilian Authors*, p. 22.

Bueno's novel identifies forthrightly with this strand of both science fiction and structural fabulation because of its postulation of a foregrounded fictive world in which semantic relations rather than "psychological" profiles are developed. *Asilo* concerns an unnamed land dominated by a group of towers, futuristic skyscrapers, that are the outward sign of a totalitarian industrial-bureaucratic society to which individuals clamor for admission but which inexorably annihilates their human qualities. Thus, the title word *asilo*, asylum, is ironic in a very obvious fashion:

> Os elevadores subiam e desciam sempre devagar; a velocidade fora calculada por um grupo de técnicos, incumbidos de acelerá-los a fim de facilitar a comunicação dos diferentes setores. O erro de cálculo nunca foi apurado, assim como também nunca foi possível acertar depois a marcha dos elevadores lentos, excessivamente lentos. Muitos cochilavam sentados, enquanto eles não vinham. Outros impacientavam-se com isso, principalmente os novos quando chegavam, e os antigos, nas horas de saída. Aos poucos, à medida que os novos passavam a antigos, adaptando-se ao ritmo do trabalho nas torres, aos tempos de espera, acostumavam-se também ao passo dos elevadores.
>
> O elevador reservado para o rei e do qual se serviam além dele os seus amigos, era mais veloz do que o raio e ele, apenas ele, chegava ao topo da torre, aquela que vivia imersa nas nuvens beirando o infinito.[33]

(The elevators went up and down slowly. Their speed was calculated by a group of technicians, charged with accelerating them in the interests of facilitating communication between the different sectors. The error in calculation was never verified, just as it was never possible to adjust later the speed of the slow—excessively slow—elevators. Many dozed sitting, waiting for them to come. Others became impatient over it, principally new people when they arrived and old people when it was time to go. After a while, as the new became the old, accommodating themselves to the work rhythm of the towers, to the periods of waiting, they too grew used to the routine of the elevators.

The elevator reserved for the king, or the one used also by his friends, was quicker than the speed of light and it, only it, would go all the way to the top of the tower, the one that was always surrounded by clouds cradling the infinite.)

---

33. *Asilo nas torres, romance*, p. 123. Further citations will be made by page number in the text.

Composed of brief vignettes (many of which have as epiphonemas short passages from the Bible) that introduce individuals who are rarely identified other than by letters of the alphabet (a detail that underscores the emphasis on structural pattern rather than plot schemata), the novel invites a reading as an elaborate metaphor for the cruel arbitrariness of the alternately chaotic and rigidly structured governments that are characteristic of Latin American dictatorships in Brazil and elsewhere in the Third World. That the world of the towers appears to be a vast "anonymizing" business enterprise only confirms the hypothesis that capitalism is a socioeconomic system that both abets and is abetted by repressive regimes in Latin America. At the same time, such a system leads to entropic decay and the gradual disintegration of a society in which all human feeling has been eliminated in favor of a tyrannical order that progresses with unreflecting and unresponsive rhythm:

> Não, ninguém entendia o que estava acontecendo. Os relatórios da segurança espantavam pelos resultados. As fissuras e a umidade que apareciam nas paredes, surgindo de repente para depois sumirem, eram fenômenos inexplicáveis. Toda a estrutura das torres fora examinada por peritos, as paredes, o sistema de refrigeração, as tubulações. Os resultados obtidos foram levados ao computador que confirmou os relatórios: nenhuma anormalidade.
>
> Apesar da apreensão que as fissuras causavam, os técnicos tranqüilizavam a todos, afirmando que da ausência de explicação para o fenômeno não decorria motivo para suspeita: as torres não corriam perigo. (p. 86)

> (No, no one understood what was going on. The security reports inspired fear for what they revealed. The cracks and moisture that had appeared in the walls, showing up suddenly and then disappearing, were inexplicable phenomena. The entire structure of the towers was examined by specialists—the walls, the cooling system, the conduits. The results thus obtained were fed into the computer, which confirmed the reports: no abnormality.
>
> Despite the concern caused by the fissures, the technicians were comforting, affirming that, in the absence of any explanation for the phenomenon, there was no motive for alarm: the towers were in no danger.)

Of course, Bueno's novel is more than transparent social allegory, particularly in the development of the antithesis between the two named characters, the bitch-goddess Salomé and the virginal Assunta. The chilling insouciance of the relentless accumulation of images of the destruction of the prized human feelings of Western humanism, feelings that often become repressed in the pursuit of both technological progress and established social order, is the basis for the dense narrative texture of this impressive novel.

It is not surprising that Brazil, a country that is both highly industrialized and representative of the sociocultural and political problems of the Third World, should have developed an important science-fiction tradition in its literature. The structuralist fabulation of postmodernist fiction seeks to develop audacious and disruptive metaphors without seeing universalist themes in terms of the psychological problems of fictional characters. Brazilian writers would appear to have found in science fiction one powerful instrument for achieving that goal and to have used it eloquently in order to make profound statements concerning Brazilian and Latin American society.

VI

Argentina has always been an extensive consumer of children's literature.[34] Major publishers have assiduously published editions of classical Spanish-language material as well as translations of an impressive variety of foreign literature, including Mother Goose and Grimm's fairy tales, the major English-language classics, and materials by widely diverse contemporary writers such as the Walt Disney Studios and Richard Scarry. By the same token, there is a significant output of books by national authors, and some of the most important figures in Argentine literature have written material for children; Argentina also has a well-developed commitment to children's theater. One attractively produced series deserves close attention, most notably for the outstanding Latin American novelists who wrote for it during its brief existence.

The Ediciones de la Flor series Libros de la Florcita was directed in the early seventies by Amelia Hannois (at the time the wife of the Paraguayan novelist Augusto Roa Bastos) and included material, handsomely illustrated, by non–Latin American authors like Ray Bradbury, Umberto Eco, Eugène Ionesco, by Latin American authors like the Chilean Fernando Alegría

---

34. Federica Domínguez Colavita, "The Current State of Children's Literature in Argentina."

and Roa Bastos, and by Argentine authors like Silvina Ocampo and Griselda Gambaro. It is significant that none of these writers is a "children's author." All are known for their serious adult literature, and their participation in the Florcita series implies that one of the goals of the publisher was to provide children with material written by major literary figures.

The publication of a children's book by a major prose writer like Augusto Roa Bastos (born in Paraguay in 1917, Roa's major literary production has taken place in Argentina; he now lives in France) presents an interesting critical dilemma. One can simply ignore the publication as unrelated to the writer's "real" work, or one can review it as an integral part of the author's literary production, taking note of its presumedly different audience.[35] Roa's *El pollito de fuego* has received little critical attention, indicating that Roa scholars have adopted the first of the two options.

If read as one reads Borges or Cortázar, *Pollito* would be called an example of magical realism: a little chicken, although normal at birth, acquires the ability to become a burning lump of feathers and cartilage, a metamorphosis that alters drastically the circumstances of life on the farm. However, after a period of fame in which the farmer and his wife become wealthy from public attention, the little chick undergoes a spell of loneliness and depression, only to experience a second metamorphosis and emerge as a resplendent blue cock that destroys a dragonlike *yarará* snake and disappears into the forest. As the narrator tells the children who form the audience within the story, Pipiolín has taken flight to seek a friend, and perhaps one of them will find him waiting in the corner of his or her own room.

Although Roa's story is an example of magical realism in its use of an expressionistic context (the ability to become a source of fire and light) and in its use of metamorphoses to provide the transition from one stage of life to another, it does not, ironically, differ from the main traditions of modern children's literature, particularly the tradition that views literature as a means for making its young audience aware of the rich texture of life and the marvelous and the mysterious that underlie everyday events. That is, children's literature may be seen as making use

---

35. For an overview of Roa's literary production, see David William Foster, *Augusto Roa Bastos*.

of myth and magical realism for approximately the same reason that adult literature does: not so much to entertain with the unusual as to enhance our perception of the complexity of the quotidian. Various modes of language innovation may be attributed to children's writing as part of its guiding conception of the relationship between event and linguistic expression:

—¡Este bicho es el demonio en forma de pollito! Hay que ahogarlo en el arroyo inmediatamente!
—¡Mándenlo a Tierra del Fuego!—corearon otros lenguas largas—. ¡Que se vaya a vivir con los pingüinos entre los hielos! ¡Que se vaya a vivir con los pingüinos entre los hielos! La familia de don Prudencio [el chacarero] no opinaba lo mismo. Se encariñaron con Pipiolín. Doña Rosa le tejió unos escarpines impermeables. Valeria, la hija mayor, le fabricó un paraguas. Cuando Pipiolín quiso usarlos se convirtieron en rulos de ceniza. Marita, la menor, que estudiaba en la ciudad, le trajo entonces un uniforme de bombero en miniatura: botas, capote, anteojos de protección y hasta un matafuego no más grande que un dedal. Marita conversaba mucho con Pipiolín. Le enseñaba lo que ella aprendía. El pollito escuchaba abriendo mucho los ojos, como si quisiera decir:
—¡Qué grande es el mundo y cuántas cosas caben en él![36]

("This animal is the devil in the form of a chick? He must be drowned in the stream immediately!"
"Send him to Tierra del Fuego," other busybodies chimed in.
"Let him go live with the penguins on the ice!"
Let him go live with the penguins on the ice! Don Prudencio's family was not of the same opinion. They had grown fond of Pipiolín. Doña Rosa knit him some little waterproof slippers. Valeria, the oldest daughter, made him an umbrella. When Pipiolín attempted to use them, they turned into curls of ash. Marita, the youngest child, who was going to school in the city, brought him a miniature fireman's outfit: boots, cape, protective goggles, and even an extinguisher no larger than a thimble. Marita talked a lot with Pipiolín. She taught him what she was studying. The little chick would listen to her with his eyes wide, as though wanting to say:
"How big the world is, and how many things there are in it!")

Pollito, nevertheless, is not fundamentally different from Roa's major fiction. If, as we find in his literature, the mythic, the magical, the *pensée sauvage* are all meant to bypass the civilized and the rational, what better vehicle than a literature in-

---

36. *El pollito de fuego*, pp. [14–15]. The illustrations are by Juan Marchesi. Further citations will be made by page number in the text.

tended for those "innocents" who have not yet had their perceptions modified by civilization and rationalization?[37] The framing of the narrative is significant in this regard. There is the storyteller who relates the tale of Pipiolín, and she and her audience of children comment on the story during various parts of the narrative. For example, one of the children corrects the storyteller for her anthropomorphizing choice of words:

> Un pompón todo rojo. De la cabeza a los pies. . .
> —A las patitas, querrás decir.
> —Bueno, sí. De la cabeza a las patitas. (p. [9])

> (A completely red pompom. From head to feet. . .
> "You mean claws."
> "Well, yes. From head to claws.")

In addition, the storyteller's narrative is contrasted with a supposed television narrative of the same or a similar event. After some discussion of the television program (illustrated in the book by twelve video frames above the narrative, the last one carrying the legend "Continuamos en 'Para Usted la Realidad'" ["Now Back to 'Reality for You'"]), the storyteller asserts "—No, chicos. Lo que pasó realmente fue . . ." ["No, children. What really happened was that . . ." (p. [7])]. This framing serves to affirm the interest of the story for the audience of children, represented in the text as the storyteller's audience, and to debunk the primacy of television coverage.

Roa's *Pollito* is both a significant departure from the bulk of his extremely difficult and somber fiction and an implicit testimonial of the variety of forms in contemporary Latin American writing. Scholarship on the Latin American narrative must be willing to go beyond its concentration on magical realism and other manifestations of the boom if it is to achieve a more comprehensive representation of creative activity in Latin America. While there has been an understandable interest in testimonial literature, an interest that is the consequence of abiding concerns for the quality of life in Latin America, other categories such as the ones studied in this chapter demand further analysis and interpretation.

---

37. Roa has maintained, rather sardonically, that "Pensar es insalubre" (to think is unhealthy) in a "Cuestionario" published in *Crisis*, no. 3 (1973):36.

Concluding Remarks

Latin Americanists, whether American, European, or Latin American, tend to agree that there is an urgent need for recasting the priorities and the parameters of Latin American studies. The dissatisfaction with what we have accomplished to date in terms of substantive research moves along several axes. First, there is a concern for identifying the proper audience for such research. Certainly, there is a need to place the study of literature and culture in the wider framework of identifying what Latin American society is and can be. This sort of sociopolitical commitment exercizes considerable influence in the choice of authors, works, and phenomena to be studied, and it explains, quite obviously, why certain segments of the Latin American literary production move in and out of favor with scholars and their research programs. Concomitantly, such a commitment explains in part why English-language Latin Americanists feel the urgency to share their study of Latin American culture in English with their own countrymen in the belief that such intercultural knowledge is of vital importance to both societies. My own response to this commitment is the basis for the decision to comment in English on a range of Latin American literary works that are in many cases precisely *not* those English-language readers are reading in translation. I therefore leave for another time the task of explaining in English only those works that the English-language reading public may be currently reading in English.

The very definition of literature constitutes another important axis of the scope of a study such as the one I have undertaken. Most readers who have any experience with contemporary writing accept that the boundaries between "literature" and other forms of cultural writing have become hopelessly blurred. It is this blurring that provides one of the most dynamic principles of contemporary cultural writing and exemplifies one of the bases for speaking of current forms of "experimental," "disruptional," or simply "innovative" writing. As I have tried to argue in my comments on such works in Latin America, not only does this blurring phenomenon allow us to expand considerably the frontiers of what we are going to call literary production in Latin America, but it is precisely these works in which we find the most original contributions of Latin American writers. It is for this reason that such works overlap so notably with the general sociopolitical concerns of intellectuals in Latin America as part of a continuous fabric of cultural writing. As a consequence, coming to terms with such works and the diversity of forms they represent implies a criterion of selection considerably different than one based on the identification of "key" or "major" Latin American works (which is a criterion that brings us back, inevitably, to those works available in English translation and the problem of whether this inventory is a reliable guide to "great" Latin American literature).

Finally, the sort of scrutiny to which the works chosen for examination are submitted is of considerable importance in the definition of an appropriate program of literary and cultural study of Latin American writing. The critical practice of a semiotic reading—the study of how texts go about setting up a process of meaning that the reader undertakes to comprehend and assimilate—is part of the commitment to understanding how cultural writing in any society, but in Latin America in particular, partakes of the generalized need for serious assessment of the conflicting ideologies of that society. The practices of cultural writing are both themselves ideological projects (conceptions of what literature can be and how it functions in a society) and particular conventionalized forms of response— as "novels," for example, or as "autobiographical," "testimonial," or "documentary" narratives, or as "essays," and so on— to the need to interpret social experience through the medium of cultural writing. Within this context, the attention to the formal aspects of writing only has critical validity if it ultimately leads to a characterization of the cultural text as one legitimate example of the construction, through the medium of writing, of a meaningful interpretation of sociocultural experience. My comments are not intended as semiotic analyses as such (this would involve a degree of formalism or formalistic metalanguage that would leave behind the general reader I hope to appeal to). Rather, comments that imply a semiological focus are intended to affirm the need to retain an emphasis on literature and cultural writing not as merely the "representation" of social experience but as a specific (re)formulation of meaning about the Latin American social experience. For this reason, I have attempted to underscore the particular writing texture of the works examined and the way in which they represent particular or important strategies in Latin American cultural writing for dealing with the complex issues of the Latin American social experience.

My personal decisions with regard to these questions concerning how to write scholarly criticism about Latin American literature must, in the final analysis, be evaluated in terms of the relative success of this study in suggesting a wider scope of interest in Latin American literary or cultural writing than has generally been available thus far in English-language studies on the subject.

Bibliography

Works Studied

Asís, Jorge. *Los reventados.* Buenos Aires: Sudamericana, 1977; Crisis, 1974.

Barnet, Manuel. *Biografía de un cimarrón.* 2d ed. Mexico City: Siglo XXI, 1971. Published in English under the title *The Autobiography of a Runaway Slave: Esteban Montejo,* trans. Jacosta Innes. London: Bodley Head, 1966; New York: Pantheon Books, 1968.

Bueno, Ruth. *Asilo nas torres, romance.* São Paulo: Atica, 1979.

Carneiro, André. *Piscina livre.* São Paulo: Moderna, 1980.

Corra, Hugo. *Frontera sin retorno.* Buenos Aires: Corregidor, 1978.

García Márquez, Gabriel. *Relato de un náufrago.* Barcelona: Tusquets, 1970.

Ibargüengoitia, Jorge. *Las muertas.* Mexico City: Joaquín Mortiz, 1977. Published in English as *The Dead Girls,* trans. Asa Zatz. New York: Avon Books, 1983.

Jorge, Miguel. *Veias e vinhos.* São Paulo: Atica, 1981.

Lastra, Héctor. *La boca de la ballena.* Buenos Aires: Corregidor, 1974.

Louzeiro, José. *Aracelli, meu amor: um anjo espera a justiça dos homens.* 4th ed. Rio de Janeiro: Record, 1981.

Lynch, Marta. *La penúltima versión de la Colorada Villanueva.* Buenos Aires: Sudamericana, 1978.

Martínez Moreno, Carlos. *El color que el infierno me escondiera.* Mexico City: Nueva Imagen, 1981.

Medina, Enrique. *Perros de la noche.* Buenos Aires: Eskol, 1977.

———. *Strip-tease.* Buenos Aires: Corregidor, 1976.

Mendoza, María Luisa. *De Ausencia.* Mexico City: Joaquín Mortiz, 1974.

Perón, Eva. *La razón de mi vida.* Buenos Aires: Peuser, 1951. Published in English as *Evita by Evita: Eva Duarte Perón Tells Her Own Story.* New York: Proteus Publishing Co., 1978.

Poniatowska, Elena. *La noche de Tlatelolco: testimonios de historia oral.* 8th ed. Mexico City: Era, 1971. Published in English as *Massacre in Mexico,* trans. Helen R. Lane. New York: Viking Press, 1975.

Puig, Manuel. *El beso de la mujer araña.* Barcelona: Seix Barral, 1976. Published in English as *Kiss of the Spider Woman,* trans. Thomas Colchie. New York: Alfred A. Knopf, 1979.

Roa Bastos, Augusto. *El pollito de fuego.* Illustrated by Juan Marchesi. Buenos Aires: Ediciones de la Flor, 1974.

Roffé, Reina. *Monte de Venus.* Buenos Aires: Corregidor, 1976.

Valdés, Hernán. *Tejas Verdes, diario de un campo de concentración en Chile.* Barcelona: Ariel, 1974.

Walsh, Rodolfo. *Operación massacre.* Buenos Aires: Jorge Alvarez, 1969.

Criticism

General References

Alemán Sainz, Francisco. *Las literaturas de kiosko.* Barcelona: Planeta/ Editora Nacional, 1975.

Amorós, Andrés. *Subliteraturas.* Barcelona: Ariel, 1974.

Avellaneda, Andrés Oscar. "El tema del peronismo en la narrativa argentina." Ph.D. diss., University of Illinois, 1973.

Barnet, Miguel. "La novela testimonio: socio-literatura." In his *La canción de Rachel,* 125–50. Barcelona: Estela, 1970.

Barthes, Roland. *S/Z.* Trans. Richard Miller. New York: Hill and Wang, 1974.

Benstock, Shari. "At the Margin of Discourse: Footnotes in the Fictional Text." *PMLA* 98 (1983):204–25.

Block de Behar, Lisa. *Análisis de un lenguaje en crisis.* Montevideo: Nuestra Tierra, 1969.

Borello, Rodolfo A. "Novela e historia: la visión fictiva del período peronista en las letras argentinas." *Anales de literatura hispanoamericana,* no. 8 (1979):29–72.

Brushwood, John S. *The Spanish American Novel: A Twentieth Century Survey.* Austin: University of Texas Press, 1975.

Carneiro, André. *Introdução ao estudo da ciência ficção.* São Paulo: Conselho Estadual de Cultura, 1967.

Carpentier, Alejo. "De lo real maravillosamente americano." In his *Tientos y differencias (ensayos),* 115–35. Mexico City: Universidad Nacional Autónoma de México, 1964.

Charney, Maurice. *Sexual Fiction.* London: Methuen, 1981.

Cirne, Moacy. "FC: A/Z." *Vozes* 70, no. 6 (1976):57–66.

Collazos, Oscar, and Julio Cortázar. *Literatura en la revolución y revolución en la literatura.* Mexico City: Siglo XXI, 1970.

"Coloquio sobre literatura chilena en la resistencia y en el exilio," *Casa de las Américas,* no. 112 (1979):73–109.

Crews, Frederick. "Anaesthetic Criticism." In his *Psychoanalysis and Literary Process,* 1–24. Cambridge, Mass.: Winthrop, 1970.

Culler, Jonathan. *Structuralist Poetics: Structuralism, Linguistics, and the Study of Literature.* Ithaca, N.Y.: Cornell University Press, 1975.

Dijk, Teun A. van. *Pragmatics of Language and Literature.* New York: American Elsevier, 1976.

Domínguez, Colavita. "The Current State of Children's Literature in Argentina." *Children's Literature* 7 (1978):169–80.

Dorfman, Ariel. *Imaginación y violencia en América*. Santiago, Chile: Editorial Universitaria, 1970.

Dunbar, David Lincoln. "Unique Motifs in Brazilian Science Fiction." Ph.D. diss., University of Arizona, 1976.

Fernández Moreno, César, comp. *América latina en su literatura*. Mexico City: Siglo XXI, 1972.

Foster, David William. *Argentine Narrative of Social Realism*. Unpublished.

———. "The Brazilian Short Story." In *The Latin American Short Story*, by Margaret Sayers Peden, 1–34. Boston: G. K. Hall, 1983.

———. *Currents in the Contemporary Argentine Novel*. Columbia: University of Missouri Press, 1975.

———. "Latin American Documentary Narrative." *PMLA* 99 (1984): 41–55.

———. "Narrativa testimonial argentina en los años del 'Proceso.'" *Plural* 2, no. 150 (1984):21–23.

———. "La problemática del lenguaje en la nueva narrativa: observaciones liminares." *Cuadernos para investigación de la literatura hispánica*, no. 5 (1983):49–59.

Foster, David William, and Luis Peña. "Materiales para el estudio de la nueva narrativa hispanoamericana: dos ensayos bibliográficos." *Revista interamericana de bibliografía*. Forthcoming.

Fuentes, Carlos. *La nueva novela hispanoamericana*. Mexico City: Joaquín Mortiz, 1969.

Goldar, Ernesto. "La literatura peronista." In *El peronismo*, 139–86. Buenos Aires: Carlos Pérez, 1969.

———. *El peronismo en la literatura argentina*. Buenos Aires: Freeland, 1971.

Hawkes, Terence. *Structuralism and Semiotics*. Berkeley: University of California Press, 1977.

Hellmann, John. *Fables of Fact: The New Journalism as New Fiction*. Urbana: University of Illinois Press, 1981.

Hollowell, John. *Fact & Fiction: The New Journalism and the Nonfiction Novel*. Chapel Hill: The University of North Carolina Press, 1977.

Iser, Wolfgang. *The Implied Reader: Patterns of Communication in Prose Fiction from Bunyan to Beckett*. Baltimore: Johns Hopkins University Press, 1974.

Jitrik, Noé. "Destrucción de formas en las narraciones." In *América en su literatura*, edited by César Fernández Moreno, 219–42.

———. *El no existente caballero: la idea de personaje y su evolución en la narrativa latinoamericana*. Buenos Aires: Megápolis, 1975.

Katra, William H. "The Argentine Generation of 1955: Politics, the Essay and Literary Criticism." Ph.D. diss., University of Michigan, 1977.

Klinkowitz, Jerome. *Literary Disruptions*. Urbana: University of Illinois Press, 1975.

Krueger, Roberto. "Abertura/apertura: A Political Review of Recent Brazilian Writings." In *The Discourse of Power: Culture, Hegemony and the Authoritarian State*, edited by Neil Larsen, 172–93. Minneapolis: Institute for the Study of Ideologies and Literature, 1983.

Langford, Walter. *The Mexican Novel Comes of Age*. Notre Dame: University of Notre Dame Press, 1971.

Larson, Ross. "La literatura de la ciencia-ficción en México." *Cuadernos hispanoamericanos*, no. 284 (1974):425–31.

Lima, Luiz Costa. *A metamorfose do silêncio*. Rio de Janeiro: Eldorado, 1974.

———. *A perversão do trapezista*. Rio de Janeiro: Imago, 1976.

Lorenz, Gunter. *Diálogo con América latina*. Santiago, Chile: Pomaire, 1972.

Lugo, Marvin d'. "Fruto de los 'frutos prohibidos': la fantaciencia rioplatense." In *Otros mundos otros fuegos*, by the Instituto Internacional de Literatura Iberoamericana, 139–44. East Lansing: Michigan State University, Latin American Studies Center, 1975.

Martínez, Miguel A. "El dictador hispanoamericano como personaje literario." *Latin American Research Review* 16, no. 2 (1981):79–105.

Mellard, James. "Prolegomena to a Study of the Popular Mode in Narrative." *Journal of Popular Culture* 6, no. 1 (1972):1–19.

Portantiero, Juan Carlos. *Realismo y realidad en la narrativa argentina*. Buenos Aires: Procyón, 1961.

Pratt, Mary Louise. *Toward a Speech Act Theory of Literary Discourse*. Bloomington: Indiana University Press, 1977.

Prieto, Adolfo. *Sociología del público argentino*. Buenos Aires: Leviatán, 1956.

Rama, Angel. "El 'boom' en perspectiva." *Escritura*, no. 7 (1979):3–45.

Reis, Roberto. "A significância ou o resgate da significação." *Suplemento literário de Minas Gerais* (2–9 July 1977):6–7.

Riffaterre, Michael. *Semiotics of Poetry*. Bloomington: Indiana University Press, 1978.

Rodríguez Monegal, Emir. *El boom de la novela hispanoamericana, ensayos*. Caracas: Tiempo Nuevo, 1972.

———. "Writing Fiction under the Censor's Eye." *World Literature Today* 53 (1979):19–22.

Rosser, Harry L. *Conflict and Transition in Rural Mexico: The Fiction of Social Realism*. Boston: Crossroads Press, 1980.

Scholes, Robert. *Structural Fabulation: An Essay on Fiction of the Future*. Notre Dame: University of Notre Dame Press, 1975.

Sibenschuh, William R. *Fictional Techniques and Factual Works*. Athens: University of Georgia Press, 1983.

Smith, Barbara Herrnstein. *On the Margins of Discourse: The Relation of Literature to Language*. Chicago: University of Chicago Press, 1978.

Stabb, Martin S. "Argentine Letters and the Peronato: An Overview." *Journal of Inter-American Studies*, nos. 3–4 (1971):434–55.

Vidal, Hernán. *Literatura hispanoamericana e ideología liberal: surgimiento y crisis (una problemática sobre la dependencia en torno a la narrativa del boom)*. Takoma Park, Md.: Hispamérica, 1976.

Weber, Ronald. *The Literature of Fact: Literary Non-Fiction in American Writing*. Athens: Ohio University Press, 1980.

White, Hayden. *Tropics of Discourse: Essays in Cultural History*. Baltimore: Johns Hopkins University Press, 1978.

Zavarzadeh, Mas'ud. *The Mythopoeic Reality: The Postwar American Nonfiction Novel*. Urbana: University of Illinois Press, 1976.

Asís

Avellaneda, Andrés. "'Best-seller' y código represivo en la narrativa argentina del ochenta: el caso Asís." *Revista iberoamericana*, no. 125 (1983):983–96.

Barnet

Barnet, Miguel. "Miguel Barnet charla con los editores de *Vórtice*." *Vórtice* 2, nos. 2–3 (1979):1–10.

Bejel, Emilio. "Entrevista: Miguel Barnet." *Hispamérica*, no. 29 (1981): 41–52.

Chang-Rodríguez, Raquel. "Sobre *La canción de Rachel*, novela-testimonio." *Revista iberoamericana* 44 (1978):133–38.

Fernández Guerra, Angel Luis. "*Cimarrón y Rachel*, un 'continuum.'" *Unión* 1, no. 4 (1970):161–67.

González Echevarría, Roberto. "*Biografía de un cimarrón* and the Novel of the Cuban Revolution." *Novel* 13 (1980):249–63.

Moreno Fraginals, Manuel. "*Biografía de un cimarrón*." *Casa de las Américas*, no. 40 (1967):131–32.

Schulman, Ivan A. "Reflections on Cuba and Its Antislavery Literature." *Southeastern Conference on Latin American Studies* 7 (1976): 59–67.

Bueno

Duarte, José Afrânio Moreira. "Ruth Bueno." In *A Dictionary of Contemporary Brazilian Authors*, edited by David William Foster and Roberto Reis, 22. Tempe: Arizona State University, Center for Latin American Studies, 1982.

Carneiro

Barrow, Leo. "André Carneiro." In *A Dictionary of Contemporary Brazilian Authors*, edited by David William Foster and Roberto Reis, 30–31. Tempe: Arizona State University, Center for Latin American Studies, 1982.

García Márquez

Ludmer, Josefina. *Cien años de soledad: una interpretación*. Buenos Aires: Tiempo Contemporáneo, 1972.

Müller-Bergh, Klaus. "*Relato de un náufrago*: Gabriel García Márquez's Tale of Shipwreck and Survival at Sea." *Books Abroad* 47 (1973): 460–66.

Ruffinelli, Jorge. "Diez días en el mar." In *Sobre García Márquez*, edited by Pedro Simón Martínez, 207–9. Montevideo: Biblioteca Marcha, 1971.

———. "Un periodista llamado Gabriel García Márquez." In his *Critica en marcha, ensayos sobre literatura latinoamericana*, 56–59. Mexico City: Premia, 1979.

Vargas Llosa, Mario. *García Márquez: historia de un deicidio*. Caracas: Monte Avila; Barcelona: Barral, 1971.

Ibargüengoitia

Bruce-Novoa, John D., and David Valentín. "Violating the Image of Violence: Ibargüengoitia's *El atentado*." *Latin American Theatre Review* 12, no. 2 (1979):13–21.

García, Gustavo. "Jorge Ibargüengoitia: la burla en primera persona." *Revista de la Universidad de México* 32, no. 12 (1978):19–23.

Ibargüengoitia, Jorge. "Memorias de novelas." *Vuelta*, no. 29 (1979): 32–34.

Jorge

Pinto, José Roberto de Almeida. "Foco narrativo—discussão sobre a nomenclatura proposta por Coelho de Carvalho, à luz de um romance de Miguel Jorge." *O popular/suplemento cultural*, no. 321 (1983):6–7.

Reali, Erilde Melillo. "Tendências da nova narrativa brasileira: *Veias e vinhos* de Miguel Jorge." *Cadernos de literatura* 13 (December 1982): 25–33.

Santos, Wendel. "Os quatro ângulos do quadrilátero: a idéia da forma e a forma da idéia em Miguel Jorge." In his *Os três reais da ficção: o conto brasileiro de hoje*, 152–62. Petrópolis: Vozes, 1978.

Lastra

Clinton, Stephen T. Review of *La boca de la ballena*. *Books Abroad* 49 (1975):86.

Louzeiro

Portão, Romão Gomes. Review of *Lúcio Flávio: o passageiro da agonia*. *Vozes* 70, no. 2 (1976):70–71.

Lynch

Birkemoe, Diane S. "The Virile Voice of Marta Lynch." *Revista de estudios hispánicos* 16, no. 2 (1982):191–211.
Flori, Monica. "El mundo femenino de Marta Lynch y Elena Poniatowska." *Letras femeninas* 9, no. 2 (1983):23–30.
Kaminsky, Amy. "Marta Lynch: The Expanding Political Consciousness of an Argentine Woman Writer." Ph.D. diss., Pennsylvania State University, 1975.
Lindstrom, Naomi. "The Literary Feminism of Marta Lynch." *Critique* 20, no. 2 (1978):49–58.
———. "Women's Discourse Difficulties in a Novel by Marta Lynch [*La señora Ordóñez*]." *I&L: Ideologies and Literature*, no. 17 (1983):339–48.
Paley de Francescato, Martha. "Marta Lynch." *Hispamérica*, no. 10 (1975):33–44.

Martínez Moreno

Benedetti, Mario. "Martínez Moreno en busca de varias certidumbres." In his *Literatura uruguaya, siglo XX: ensayo*, 174–94. 2d ed., enl. Montevideo: Alfa, 1969.
D'Aquino, Alfonso. "La novela que el cielo nos enviara." *Revista de la Universidad de México* 36, no. 3 (1981):43–46.
Rodríguez Monegal, Emir. "Las ficciones de Martínez Moreno." In his *Literatura uruguaya del medio siglo*, 260–92. Montevideo: Alfa, 1966.

Medina

Bazán, Juan F. "Enrique Medina." In his *Narrativa paraguaya y latinanoamericana*, 259–73. Asunción, 1976.
Clinton, Stephen T. "Censorship, Human Rights under Videla." *Latin American Digest* 12, no. 2 (1978):1–2.
———. "Enrique Medina." In *A Dictionary of Contemporary Latin American Authors*, edited by David William Foster, 65–66. Tempe: Arizona State University, Center for Latin American Studies, 1975.
Foster, David William. "Bare Words and Naked Truths." *The American Hispanist*, no. 12 (1976):17–19.
———. Review of *Las muecas del miedo*. *World Literature Today* 56 (1982): 309–10.
———. "Narrativa argentina en los años del 'Proceso.'" *Plural*, 2d series, no. 150 (1984):21–23.
Jozef, Bella. "Enrique Medina, o tempo sem recuperação." In her *O jogo mágico*, 119–20. Rio de Janeiro: Livraria José Olympio, 1980.

Mendoza

Bearse, Grace M. "Entrevista con María Luisa Mendoza." *Hispania* 64 (1981):459.

Castedo-Ellerman, Elena. "¿Feminismo o femineidad? Seis escritoras opinan." *Américas* 30, no. 10 (1978):19–24.

Castellanos, Rosario. "María Luisa Mendoza, el lenguaje como instrumento." In her *Mujer que sabe latín*, 165–70. Mexico City: SepDiana, 1979.

Foster, David William. "Algunos espejismos eróticos." *Revista de la Universidad de México*, no. 37 (1983):36–38.

Maiz, Magdalena. "Tres escritoras: Garro/Castellanos/Mendoza." *Plural*, no. 142 (1983):62–65.

Tatum, Charles M. Review of *De Ausencia*. *Chasqui* 5, no. 1 (1975): 54–55.

———. "María Luisa Mendoza, atrevida novelista mexicana." *Letras femeninas* 3, no. 2 (1977):31–39.

Young, Dolly J., and William D. Young. "The New Journalism in Mexico: Two Women Writers [Mendoza and Elena Poniatowska]." *Chasqui* 12, nos. 2–3 (1983):72–80.

Perón

Albornoz de Videla, Graciela. *Evita: libro de lectura para 1 grado inferior*. Buenos Aires: L. Lasserre, 1953.

Barager, Joseph R. *Why Perón Came to Power: The Background to Peronismo in Argentina*. New York: Alfred A. Knopf, 1968.

Cantarella, Adelina. *Guía para análisis analógico de "La razón de mi vida" de Eva Perón*. Buenos Aires: Librería Perlado, 1954.

Ciria, Alberto. "Flesh and Fantasy: The Many Faces of Evita (and Juan Perón)." *Latin American Research Review* 18, no. 2 (1983):150–65.

Eva Perón. Cuadernos de *Crisis*, no. 7. Buenos Aires: Noroeste, 1974.

Fischer-Pap, Lucia. *Eva: Theodora. Evita Perón: Empress Theodora Incarnated*. Rockford, Ill.: LFP Publications, 1982.

Goldar, Ernesto. "Eva Perón: una filosofía de la historia." In his *La descolonización ideológica*, 127–33. Buenos Aires: A. Peña Lillo, 1973.

Kapschutschenko, Ludmila. "Evita y el feminismo: mito y realidad." *Letras femeninas* 9, no. 1 (1983):43–52.

Katra, William. "Eva Perón: Media Queen of the Peronist Working Class." *Revista/Review interamericana* 11 (1981):238–51.

———. "Eva Perón: Popular ♡ueen of Hearts." *Latin American Digest* 14, no. 2 (1980):6–7, 19–20.

Liberal, José R. *Eva Perón: estudio literario y valoración sociológica de "La razón de mi vida."* Buenos Aires: Espiño, 1953.

Sebreli, Juan José. *Eva Perón ¿aventurera o militante?* 4th ed., enl. Buenos Aires: La Pleyade, 1971.

Taylor, J. M. *Eva Perón: The Myths of a Woman*. Chicago: University of Chicago Press, 1979.

Weber, Andrew Lloyd, and Tim Rice. *Evita: The Legend of Evita Perón (1919–1952)*. New York: Avon, 1979.

Wilkie, James W., and Monica Menell-Kinberg. "*Evita*: From Elitelore to Folklore." *Journal of Latin American Lore* 7, no. 1 (1981):99–140.

Poniatowska

Christ, Ronald. "The Author as Editor." *Review, Center for Inter-American Relations*, no. 15 (1975):78–79.

Flori, Monica. "El mundo femenino de Marta Lynch y Elena Poniatowska." *Letras femeninas* 9, no. 2 (1983):23–30.

Fox-Lockert, Lucía. "Elena Poniatowska." In her *Women Novelists of Spain and Spanish America*, 260–77. Metuchen, N.J.: Scarecrow Press, 1979.

Franco, Jean. "The Critique of the Pyramid and Mexican Narrative after 1968." In *Latin American Fiction Today: A Symposium*, edited by Rose S. Minc, 49–60. Takoma Park, Md.: Hispamérica; Upper Montclair, N.J.: Montclair State College, 1979.

Leal, Luis. "Tlatelolco, Tlatelolco." *Denver Quarterly* 14, no. 1 (1979): 3–13.

Miller, Beth, and Alfonso González. "Elena Poniatowska." In their *26 autoras del México actual*, 299–321. Mexico City: Costa-Amic, 1978.

Paz, Octavio. *Posdata*. Mexico City: Siglo XXI, 1970. Published in English as *The Other Mexico: Critique of the Pyramid*, trans. Lysander Kemp. New York: Grove Press, 1972.

Poniatowska, Elena. "Un libro que me fue dado." *Vida literaria*, no. 3 (1970):3–4.

Starčević, Elizabeth. "Elena Poniatowska: Witness for the People." In *Contemporary Women Authors of Latin America*, 72–77. Brooklyn: Brooklyn College Press, 1983.

Young, Dolly J., and William D. Young. "The New Journalism in Mexico: Two Women Writers [Poniatowska and María Luisa Mendoza]." *Chasqui* 12, nos. 2–3 (1983):72–80.

Puig

Epple, Juan Armando. "Bibliografía de Manuel Puig y sobre él." *Revista interamericana de bibliografía* 28 (1978):165–68.

Roa Bastos

Foster, David William. *Augusto Roa Bastos*. Boston: G. K. Hall/Twayne, 1978.

———. "Augusto Roa Bastos's *I the Supreme*: The Image of a Dictator." *Latin American Literary Review*, no. 7 (1975):31–35.

Miliani, Domingo. "El dictador: objeto narrativo en *Yo el Supremo*." *Revista de crítica literaria latinoamericana*, no. 4 (1976):103–19.

Roffé

Masiello, Francine R. "Contemporary Argentine Fiction: Liberal (Pre)texts in a Reign of Terror." *Latin American Research Review* 16, no. 2 (1981):218–24.

Valdés

Epple, Juan Armando. "Esa literatura que surge de un cerco de púas." *Literatura chilena en el exilio* 2, no. 1 (1978):7–8.
Massey, Kenneth W. "From behind the Bars of Signifiers and Signifieds." *Dispositio*, no. 4 (1977):87–92.

Walsh

Ford, Anibal. "Walsh: la reconstrucción de los hechos." In *Nueva novela latinoamericana*, edited by Jorge Lafforgue, 2: 272–322. Buenos Aires: Paidós, 1969–1972.
Rama, Angel. "Rodolfo Walsh: el conflicto de culturas en Argentina." *Escritura*, no. 2 (1976):279–301.
Viñas, David. "Déjenme hablar de Walsh." *Boletín literario* (Buenos Aires), no. 1 (1982):2–3.

Index